Challenges
for the
College Bound

Challenges
for the
College Bound

*Advice and Encouragement
from a College President*

JAY L. KESLER

Baker Books
A Division of Baker Book House Co
Grand Rapids, Michigan 49516

Published by Baker Books
a division of Baker Book House Company
P.O. Box 6287, Brand Rapids, MI 49516-6287

Printed in the United States of America

Library of Congress Cataloging-in-Publication Data

Kesler, Jay.
  Challenges for the college bound: advice and encouragement from a college president / Jay L. Kesler.
    p.   cm.
  Includes bibliographical references.
  ISBN 0-8010-5262-9
    1. College students—Religious life. 2. Christian life—1960-
BV4531.2.K4583 1994
248.8'34—dc20   93-36779

Contents

Introduction

Many of the world's cultures have a ceremony of some kind that marks the transition from childhood or adolescence to adulthood. Some of these are primitive and painful and involve frightening initiation rites such as body disfigurement, tests of strength or courage, proof of hunting skills, memorization of religious books, and respect for taboos.

The closest thing to all of this in America is high school graduation. Fortunately it is not as painful nor are you expected to jump right into adult responsibilities of marriage, family, and vocation, especially if you choose to go to college. While it is true that some find the challenge of college more difficult than do others because of economic factors, family situations, high school records, or even personal motivation, in the United States so many options are available that almost anyone who desires a college education can get one. I am not saying that it is easy, nor will it happen without planning and perseverance, yet there are more opportunities than you might realize. One purpose of this book is to explore these possibilities.

When you graduate you will begin to experience new freedoms that were not available to you as a child. This will be especially true if you go away to college in another city or state. For students who stay at home, the desire for independence is one of the tension points between them and their parents. You will become much more in control of your own time. Parents will no longer encourage you to get enough sleep or make sure you have allowed enough time to get ready for a morning appointment. We will explore this new freedom in this book.

You will be accountable before God for your own conduct for the most part. If, for example, you want to be deceptive and irresponsible in your sexual behavior, there will be no one to force you to behave. During the next few years you will become a self-regulated adult. You will have to decide if God is going to figure into this process, and if so, how.

As you become more independent from your family, you will have to decide what values will guide your life, how to manage your money, what food you will eat, and how to manage your leisure time. This is not simply a matter of getting out of high school and entering a time of freedom and relaxation. It is also the beginning of a new chapter called adulthood. It is a time of intellectual development, decision-making, and becoming the person God had in mind when he created you.

I have spent my entire adult life working with young people. In this book I am passing on to you my best insights in all of these areas. To do the best job possible, I have asked for the help of several student, friends, a few years older than you, to tell you what they wish they had known before they went to college and began developing their adult lives. All of these students are what we would term successful, though they are quite different in personality type and aspirations. Some are more into the social scene. One is an outstanding athlete who decided to drop out of varsity sports to pursue singing. All are serious about their Christian lives but come from diverse church backgrounds. They have attended both Christian and secular schools. Some have had to work almost full time to pay their bills and some have been able to spend vacations on overseas study and work programs. I'm confident that if you met them you would feel good about listening to them. In each chapter I've included their best suggestions on each subject to help you in your decision-making process.

Congratulations! You've graduated from high school so now let's commence the next chapter of your life. Welcome to young adulthood.

1

Independence

Very few desires accompany graduation with greater intensity than the one for independence. Every generation has experienced it, and your experience is no different from the rest. At some time when young adults realize they are growing from childhood to adulthood, they come to a place where they want their parents to cut them some slack. They feel like the person seen on a thousand television ads who says in effect, "Mother, I want to be me!" The young adults are really saying that they've trusted their folks up to a certain point, watched them live their lives, listened to their values, gone where they wanted them to go, for the most part have been a cooperative part of the family, and now have a great urge to say,

"You can't believe how badly I wanted to get out on my own! It wasn't that I hated my folks or anything. In fact, I loved them and I love them now. What I really wanted was to be on my own and be my own person and try out my own ideas without anyone telling me what to do. I didn't really care that much about where I went to college, just so it was away from home. I came here because my folks liked the school and felt it was a good place for me. I was sure as soon as they left me that first day that I would do things they wouldn't exactly approve of, yet I didn't want to be immoral or anything. I love college and I am pretty much on my own, even though my folks pay my college expenses. Now I realize that independence is not all I thought it was. I've learned to discipline myself in ways that my folks never could have convinced me to do. I guess I've found out more about responsibility and I'm kind of proud of the way I live. I think my folks are, too."

"I need some freedom. I want independence. I need to run my own life."

Often in talking with parents about this issue, I use the illustration of "Mother England." England had many colonies around the world. When England was a young parent she had a colony in the New World called America. America kept asking for more and more independence, and Mother England kept twisting the thumbscrews tighter and tighter, coming up with more restrictions and laws and greater control and finally a tax on tea. You'll remember from your school lessons how a group of American patriots dumped a whole load of tea in the Boston harbor, something we've come to know as the Boston Tea Party. This was an act of rebellion on the part of Mother England's children. As a result, tensions rose, and eventually a full-fledged family fight developed into the American Revolution.

Looking back on all of this, a lot of people have wondered if this war was really necessary, because we have examples all over the world of children of Mother England who did not have a revolution. I often use the illustration of India, another country in England's empire, which worked together with the governing country and over a period of time developed laws and infrastructure and ways of going about things, especially the civil-service tradition, that allowed India to have independence without costly revolution.

I use this as a simple illustration to parents to help them understand that the desire for independence is natural for everyone, especially their teenagers, and you understand this even better than they do. That urge comes not only from what you think but from deep within you. It's the desire at gut level that says, "I want to try things for myself. I want to be independent. I want to be free of my family. I want to be myself and not just part of a family blob any longer. I need to develop my own characteristics. I think I know how the world works, and I want to show people that I can make life work."

Sometimes teens try this through various things that cause tensions while they are in high school. You might decide to wear certain clothes or cut your hair a certain way to fit in with your friends at school. Parents may think that these things are associated with something evil or some group that they feel is wrong. You know that for the most part it is just your way of saying that you want to be independent from your parents and do your own thing for a while.

Following high school graduation it becomes much more possible to be independent, especially if you choose to go away from your home to college, or if you get an apartment and a job to support yourself, thus proving to your parents that you are capable of independent living. Interestingly enough, fulfilling this desire for independence in today's culture is much more difficult than it was during your parents' time. For them it was not at all uncommon for a couple to marry the summer after graduation. The young man would get a job in a local factory and the woman would get pregnant shortly thereafter. Within the year they were parents themselves, and life would begin. Today's demands on young people are much greater than this. In fact, current statistics show that the typical woman is about twenty-four years old when she marries today and the average man is about twenty-seven. The reason for this is that society puts greater demands on young people than it used to because they need more preparation before they can secure a job. The high-paying, factory-based jobs have moved overseas and people in other countries are doing this work at lower pay. The need for unskilled workers in highly paid manufacturing jobs is growing smaller.

We call today the information age. It demands that people work more with their heads than their hands and so must develop the skills and abilities not only to handle more complex machinery and equipment—computers and other communication devices—but to think discriminately and make choices based not only on one or two factors but on the evaluation of complex interrelated factors. Today's workplace requires social skills and the ability to work as a part of a team with competence and harmony.

As you now face independence as a young person in the last decade of the twentieth century, your task is slightly different from that of those who have gone before you. This is not to say people cannot make it on their own with great effort and a great deal of personal determination to make a success of life. It is, however, far better to look at your emerging independence and ask yourself if you want this to be an abrupt thing—a kind of war with your parents in which you go out and try to defy all that they and conventional wisdom have taught you—or if it is wiser to go more slowly and plan your independence so that you don't have to do it through a revolution.

I remember a touching moment with a young man recently. I spoke to a group of singles at a church and afterward saw this young man hanging around wanting some private time with me. As everyone began leaving, I turned to him and asked if I could help him in any way. He replied that he wanted to talk with me about a few things. "I'm not like all these other people. I attend this singles group occasionally because these are my friends, but I'm married. I'm caught halfway between. They are single and going to college and are home for vacation or commute, but I got married right out of high school. The truth is I had to get married, because my girlfriend was pregnant. It isn't that I don't love my wife; I love her very much. In fact, we have two children now." He pulled out pictures and showed me. He then said, "I wish as you talk with young people you would tell them that they can make it. I'm making it, but it's very hard. I work at the local supermarket. I have worked my way up from a bagger to assistant manager in the produce department. I'm learning about produce, and perhaps someday I'll be the produce manager. And who knows? If I stick with it I may become the store manager, but the pay is minimum wage. I can hardly live on what they do pay, but my dream is that someday I will make enough to be successful. If only I had thought it through and not felt as though I knew everything and got in such a hurry, life would be so different."

We talked about his relationship with Christ and whether or not he had seen his premarital sex as a sinful thing. He assured me he did and felt he had settled it between himself and God. However, the problem was he had moved into independent life without a lot of thought, and as a result he was struggling with at least two things (and I could see a third one lurking in the background). He was trying to enter the marketplace without any skill, and he was trying to work his way up—sort of lift himself up by the bootstraps. This is possible, but it certainly is not the easiest way to do it. Though being the manager of a supermarket is a worthy goal, I'm not sure it will be attainable by him, because probably someone with a business degree will be hired and get the job he is working for. He will learn a lesson we all eventually learn: Life is not fair.

The second thing is that he was in too big a hurry about his sexuality, and through decisions made in moments of passion found himself to be a father. This, of course, is an additional burden. Marriage is one thing; parenthood is quite another. While two could live as cheaply as one according to yesteryear's romantics, in real life it's not true. Marriage can be more expensive than living single, and when you add a baby, it is terribly expensive.

The problem I saw lurking in the background was his desire to be with his single friends. He obviously had not matured to the point that marriage was comfortable. He left his pregnant wife at home with the baby to carry on her responsibilities. She had no choice, after all, because the baby was almost totally dependent on her. He was reaching out to his single friends, desiring to do what they did, go where they went, and be a part of their lives. I realized that though his intentions were not malicious, and I thought he was a fine young man, this was a very difficult situation for him.

You are at a time in life where you are becoming independent. Planning what kind of independence you want is a very important part of the process. It is not necessary that it involve a revolution between you and your parents. Each fall when the freshmen arrive at Taylor University I talk with them and their parents. One of the things I try to emphasize is that though they are entering into a new chapter of life, leaving home and beginning to make a thousand choices that have been made for them before, they still are a part of their family and they still need the support and help of their parents. While it is true that now that they are away from home they can pretty well determine their own behaviors and lifestyles, it is foolish to assume that everything their parents believe and encourage is out-of-date and unworkable. Relying on parents and their advice is not a sign of immaturity. It is simply a good thing to be surrounded by caring persons. Everyone who succeeds in life does so not only through their own efforts but also through the help of others.

In the business world they call this practice networking. Throughout life you will continually develop a network of friends and trusted colleagues who will help you succeed. At this stage of your life you have classmates who care about you and may remain lifelong friends. However, the group you can really count on is your family unit. Your family who surrounds you, right back to your grandma and grandpa, if you're fortunate enough to have both sets, are a foundational group. Your parents care about you more than any other group of people on the face of the earth. In addition, you have siblings with whom you may have felt a good deal of competition up to this point, but now you will begin to see them as friends.

My family has reached an age where I can see this really working out. I remember when they were high school age my son and two daughters did a good deal of squabbling with each other, carrying out their obligation to be what all the books about families call sibling rivals. They were in competition with one another. At one time, in sort of desperation, I talked with an older friend and said, "I hope I get through this stage of high school years where the kids are doing so much squabbling and arguing with one another."

He said, "Oh, just hang on. Wait a little while. When they get into their twenties they'll become closest friends." It did turn out like that. They now are very good friends. My daughters keep very close tabs on their brother as he does on them. They are married yet interdependent on one another in a wonderful way.

As you think about your independence, don't burn all your bridges behind you or force yourself to do something silly to prove your independence. You can move ahead by developing some planned independence that will really be worthwhile.

Deep down, most parents realize this has to happen, though for many it is a traumatic experience to let go of their children. The goal of parenthood is the children's independence, but many parents get a lot of their meaning from their relationships with their children. It is terribly hard to see a child grow up. That's why dads sit at children's weddings and listen to someone sing "Sunrise, Sunset" and have tears drip from their chins. Men who've never cried before, cry at a daughter's wedding as they realize the little girl they used to hold on their lap is now a woman. It signals to them a sense of a new chapter in their life and loss for which they were not prepared.

One way to gain independence is to prove to your parents that you can handle it. The way you manage your time, your money, your health, and your relationships with others, will send strong signals to your parents that you are ready for independence. Maturity has been defined as the ability to postpone gratification. All of you know friends who don't postpone anything. They must have it all now. Because of this they often do things hastily, have experiences too early, and find themselves burned out when in fact, they should be ready to enter life rather than feel it is all over in their early twenties.

As you begin to mature and become more independent, and as your parents become more able to accept your maturity and allow you independence, some great rewards are awaiting you. One of the greatest is what I call "level" conversation. Sometime after you graduate and during your college years, you will have a level conversation with your parents. For you young men it's a very rewarding moment when for the first time you talk with your dad and you don't feel as though you are standing there in a diaper with him looking down at you as if he remembers you "bottoms up." When he sits with you and asks your opinion and you talk across the table as young adult to older adult, this is the part of freedom that is really fun. You trade a dependent relationship on your parents for a mature, adult relationship that involves sharing. This will begin a process that will be very interesting throughout your whole life, and eventually you reach a certain stage when you find yourself parenting your own parents. That is, you will be providing much of their care and making decisions for them, just as they did for you when they were stronger and you were the weaker person. This is the way the cycle of life works. It is always changing and all a part of God's plan.

As you read this book and think about independent living, consider the advice by college students given with the hope that not everyone has to touch the stove to see if it's hot. If you listen to some of the things they have learned through their move toward maturation and their urge for independence, you can have a smoother path from those teenage years through graduation into young adulthood.

Most people need all the help they can get. In fact, one of the reasons parents often seem overprotective and offer too much advice is because they have experienced pain in making bad decisions and want to spare their children that experience. But don't be afraid of making mistakes. They made them, and you will. This is called experience. What you want to do is avoid every foolish mistake that you possibly can, and in the cases where that's impossible, to profit from your errors. Keep in mind that someday you, too, will be talking to your own children and telling them what you think are the best ways to go about living life. At this point you may say that you won't do it the way your folks have done it. Perhaps not; maybe you'll be a whole lot wiser. My guess is that you may make some of the same mistakes and for the same reasons, that you will love your children and won't want them to be hurt but want them to develop independently without going through certain unnecessary agonies.

One of the ways you may insure that this process is a smoother one is to attempt to develop your own skills at communication. Find a time when you can be alone with the parent you find it easiest to talk to. Most teenagers feel that one parent is more open than the other. This parent then is often able to communicate to the other parent and pave the way for your communication with both. Perhaps the time will be as you are in a boat fishing with your dad, doing chores around the house, walking in the supermarket with your mom, taking a trip someplace in the car, or just sitting around in the kitchen when no one else is around and can begin to talk about your future. "Mom (Dad), I'm really looking forward to life now that I'm graduating, and I've been thinking about my plans for the future." Tell them what your goals and ideas are for your life. Tell them something about your values, what you feel are good things and things to be avoided. Tell them what you feel is fulfilling for you and what would make you happy. Don't be self-conscious about sharing your dreams. They, too, have had dreams, and only people who have dreamed have ever achieved great things.

One thing that makes parents overprotective and apprehensive is if they are left in the dark. They don't know how you think on certain issues, what your values are, or how you would behave in certain unsupervised situations, so they try to maintain control. If you will bother to tell them how you feel about things such as alcohol, human sexuality, honesty, and values, if they know something about your goals and dreams, then they can discuss things with you rather than feel they have to constantly warn you ahead of time about things you've already thought through very well. After all, how would they know how you feel unless you take the time to tell them?

Independence, after all, is not about being alone. It's about being a self-regulating person, a person who is able to manage his or her own life in concert with the lives of other people and to live in harmony. While there is a great urge in all of us for independence, what we really end up with is a kind of interdependence, whereby our independence interacts with other people's to create a harmonious culture. The person who says, "I don't care about anyone else. I just want to be left alone to do my thing. I don't care what you do or think!" is neither very wise nor very honest. We obviously need each other, including our families, and we all really do care about what others think about us. What we don't want to be is a puppet on a string or be manipulated by others toward their goals. We want a chance to test our wings and see how well we can do on our own.

Everyone wants to experience life. Remember when you were just a little kid and your dad took you out to fly a kite? He got the kite in the air eventually, and then you said, "Let me hold the string. I want to do it myself." He warned you not to let go of the string and perhaps tied it around your wrist. Remember how much fun it was to hold the string and feel like you were in charge of that kite way up in the sky while you were on the ground? You felt ever so grown up and independent. This is the feeling God intends us all to have. He wants us to feel that we are fulfilling the reason he created us. By the same token, he doesn't want us to let go of the string and lose the whole thing.

Now that you've graduated you are about to have more independence than you've ever dreamed possible. How you manage it, what you do with it, how well it turns out is, to a great degree, a matter of the choices you make. This book will discuss some of the choices available to students growing up in America during this particular decade. I trust you will see some wonderful opportunities, especially as you compare your ideas with the ideas the college students shared with me. I trust you will feel better prepared to move out with confidence into your own world.

Choices come with independence. Now that you are your own person and have more control over your life, it becomes evident that the choices that were previously made for you by your parents are going to be made by you. But the thing that will hit you like a bucket of cold water is that in reality a lot of choices will not really be made by you but by certain circumstances surrounding you, and the circumstances will change according to the choices you make.

As you face maturity you will also discover that life is much more like a game of chess than a simple game of Chinese checkers. There are many more options and much more happening around you; therefore, the choices you make are interdependent and important to you. For the graduate there are four major choices during this chapter of life, and how you make them will determine greatly the way the game is played the rest of your life. These choices, though they may seem frightening to think about, will all be made pretty much during your next four or five years.

First, you will decide whether or not you will go to college, and if so, what kind of college. Second, you will make a choice about your vocation—how you are going to earn a living, how you are going to support your independence and achieve your dreams based on the sort of life's work you choose, and how fulfilling it will be. Third, during these four or five years you likely will choose a life mate. With whom will you share your life? What kind of a person should you choose? What kind of dreams and aspirations does he or she have for the future, and should you get married at all? Finally, the Christian person always asks, Does God play a part in this? Am I going to allow God to dictate anything about my future, and how can I know what plans he may have for my life? Or am I going to live my life independently and do with it as I please?

These four decisions will constitute the foundation of growing up, and how they are made will say much about what your adult life will look like and what form it will begin to take.

When I discussed these issues with college students, they made the following suggestions, which I find extremely practical and insightful.

"First, realize that different is not necessarily bad. There may be several good ways to do things and to approach a subject. Be prepared in college to have your values shaken and be willing to reshuffle some of your ideas, but don't just jump on every new and novel thing that comes along. Learn to hold a suspended judgment, that is, learn to listen without making up your mind on everything. Store certain ideas away in your mind and mull them over until you really understand them, and don't be afraid to question even seemingly smart people who intimidate you. Even bright people can be wrong, or partly so. Be curious without being obstinate. All questions don't need answers right now. Hold your ground, even if the majority seems to be going the other way. If it's true, it will stand the test of time."

"Be honest with your parents about your choices. Accountability is not being a child again. All people are accountable when it comes down to it, and who really cares more than your parents? What we really want is independence and respect. Sometimes we just have to tell our parents that we understand their point of view and respect them, but we also have a point of view as well and appreciate very much their respecting it. Perhaps we will change our minds, but in the meantime, to disagree is not to be disrespectful. Tell your parents that you understand that independence and accountability go together. When you make a mistake, admit it and be willing to pay the price, even to ask for clarification and advice. Most parents won't hold this over your head. They understand that this is part of growing up."

"Get involved in an accountability group as soon as you can. Most college students want to have someone to test their ideas on. It's a good idea to find a peer group that shares your Christian faith and studies the Bible and prays together regularly. If we are really friends, we want to help each other as the Bible says: 'Bear one another's burdens, and so fulfill the law of Christ' (Gal. 6:2). If we commit ourselves to being honest with each other, and if we are willing to be open and vulnerable, we can keep each other from getting into trouble. Solomon said that in the multitude of counselors there is safety. We can help one another be strong. My friends and I often repeat to each other the fact that a three-stranded cord cannot be broken. Just because you are away from home doesn't mean that you are alone. God is always there, and so are your Christian friends. Also, don't neglect being part of a local church. That can help a lot."

2

What Does God Want of Me?

T he Bible begins with the phrase, "In the beginning God created the heavens and the earth" (Gen. 1:1). From this, certain things logically follow. First of all, if God created the world and all that's in it, and I'm obviously in it, therefore, I must have been part of God's creation. If this is true, I must have something to do with his plan. He must have made me for a purpose or reason; therefore, my life must not be totally my own to do with as I please but has something to do with his purposes for creating me. This has been the quest and dilemma of all humanity. Who am I? What am I? Why am I here? For what reason did God put me on the face of the earth?

"I used to think that maybe God had us all hooked up to some giant computer, and even though we thought we were doing our own thing, he was actually pushing all the buttons. Now I see the world to be so much more full of options. I still believe that God is in charge, but in a different way. I'm learning more about my choices and how they affect me and those around me. What scares me is that I'm afraid I'll miss what God wants or that I'll be afraid to be obedient. I also want to have fun, and sometimes I wonder if God knows all of the things I want to do with my life and then will tell me to do the opposite. I don't want to be in business like my dad, but I'm afraid maybe that's what I should do. I want to be more of a free person, yet I know that takes money. Sometimes I wish I could close my eyes and it would be twenty years from now and all the choices would be behind me. Anyway, this business of my desires and God's will is a big thing for me these days."

We understand from the Bible that God has not only created the whole world and everything in it, including us, but that God is a personal God who is very concerned about our lives and desirous that we know him and have a personal relationship with him. He does not force this relationship on us but makes it possible for us to know him through his Son, Jesus Christ. We are encouraged to put our faith and confidence and trust in Jesus Christ as our Savior, who promises to forgive our sins and to maintain our relationship with God. Sometimes, if we've been raised in the church or have grown up around Christian teaching all of our lives, we take this for granted. If young Christians are not careful, they can go into adulthood without intentionally making God part of their daily living. Now that you are moving into adulthood and are going to be much more independent, it is important to decide if you are going to allow God to be in your life what he intends to be.

Many verses in the Bible talk about this relationship. In one place God said he's "a friend who sticks closer than a brother" (Prov. 18:24). That is, he desires to walk along with us and be our guide and friend as well as our Savior and Creator. A young man who was ready to make the transition in the fall to college said to me, "I've been raised in a Christian home and I've even gone to Christian schools all my life, but I have a deep suspicion that my relationship with God is about fifteen inches from reality." I asked what he meant by that and he said, "Well, that's about the distance between my head and my heart. I understand everything about God, and I could pass any test they could give me in church about my catechism. I know all of the important events, the names of Jesus' mother and father and the disciples and the books of the Bible. I can quote several verses, but I don't think this information really has sunk into my heart. I want that to happen. I want to let Christ become the center of my life. I want him to take over the steering wheel. I want him to live in my life in a real way. I want my faith to be that kind of a real faith."

This young man's decision will make all the difference. This is true in all of our lives. When you live in your parents' home within the confines of the family structure, often you take these things for granted. When you begin to live independently, surrounded by people whose backgrounds are very different from yours, people for whom God is not even an idea but a remote concept off in space somewhere, you have to decide if you are going to live for God in a real way or if you are going to try to absorb your ideas from your culture and become just one more person who is a product of society.

I think it would be a very wise thing as any young person begins the path into adulthood to think seriously about his or her faith and ask, Is this faith really my own or is it something that I've taken for granted or inherited? This is not the time for theological discussions as to how God views it, because most likely God is much more accepting of your failures than you are; however, it is very important that you know where you stand with God and have made an overt personal decision to allow Jesus Christ to enter into your every decision and guide you through each day.

I remember in college meeting a young lady who was very impressive to me. She said, "I've learned to get up daily and say, 'This is the day the Lord has made. I will rejoice in it and be glad.' Before I let my feet hit the floor, I turn my days over to Christ and ask him to control them and be at the core of everything I think and decide and everything I do."

Making sure that you ask Christ to be in control of your life is certainly the first step of planning your future. Closely akin to this decision to accept Christ into your life as your Savior and to want him to be your companion and guide is to acknowledge that he doubtless knows more about the future, your capacities, what would make you happy, what you are fitted to do, and what you will be successful in doing than anyone else. Including God in your future plans is as important as including him in your daily life. It's important to make the will of God part of your life so that you don't find yourself living a life that is simply reactive to the world around you and being a pawn to your environment and drives.

In the large sense, it is God's will that you commit yourself to him, that you allow his revealed plan to be your plan, that you allow his Son to be your Savior, and that you crown him Lord of life in your daily activities. In the day-to-day business of making decisions and making the right choices, sometimes people wonder how they can bring God into them in the most meaningful way. I have been helped over the years by the example of a great Christian leader of the past, George Mueller. He is known among Christians as a man who served a great many children by running an orphanage and providing for them with great faith. He once spoke on making decisions that God will bless, which involves the following five steps.

First, decide to have no will of your own in the matter. This is a place in your life where you are willing to say, "Lord, I'll do anything you want me to do." Because you believe in God's essential character and knowledge, because you trust that God can handle all of the affairs of life, that he loves you enough to want you to be happy, that he desires the best, not the worst, for you, that he desires that you succeed, not fail, you can cast all your care upon him and say, "God, I have no will of my own in the matter. What do you want me to be?" Many people say this, but add, "Lord, I'll do what you want me to do, but . . . Anything except . . ." You must come without any "buts" or "excepts" and believe that God knows best. I'm convinced that there is no place to be so happy as in God's will. He will not direct you to do something that you are unable to do.

Second, Mueller suggests that you read your Bible and ask God to speak through his revealed Word. God will never lead you to do something contrary to his word. He would not lead you to be a thief or a murderer or a deceiver or a liar. As you study the Word, you will deduce the character of God and desire to imitate him rather than do things that are outside of his will. This is why it is important to develop regular Bible study habits—not to please others but to know God better.

I read in a newspaper a while back where a man was going to sell a suitcase full of drugs in Florida so he could get enough money to do something good for God. This is a contradiction. It is impossible to please God by doing something wrong to be able to do something good.

Third, George Mueller said you should pray to the Holy Spirit to guide you through the impressions of life. Some people call this self-talk, the voice that speaks within your heart. Ask God to speak to and guide you, waiting for his guidance and his voice so that, like an airplane coming to a tower signal, you get to hear the beep, beep, beep of God saying, "This is the right way," or "This is the wrong way." All Christians know what this means. If they are getting ready to do something wrong, that still small voice tells them it is a wrong move, and they begin feeling uncomfortable. They begin to have doubts about their behavior. When they do well, they sense God telling them it is the right thing to do. They gain strength they weren't aware of when God shows them they are on the right track.

Fourth, Mueller suggests that you seek objective counsel, that is, go to people who know you very well and ask them what they feel about your decision. Is it a good one, in their opinion, or a bad one? Friends are often more objective about you than you are about yourself. They know things about you that somehow you miss about your own life. People can be somewhat self-deluding sometimes and not have a good picture of who they are, but friends can tell them if they think they are able to do a certain thing. It is important to seek counsel from people who are also Christians, because God can also speak to them. Secular counselors can be of value but are often at war with God in their inner selves and unable to be objective on spiritual matters.

I remember a young man of the church who practiced the guitar for several months and then volunteered to play a solo at church. Frankly, it was a very pathetic performance. He came to me afterward in the church parking lot and said, "What do you think?"

I replied, "I'm not saying that you couldn't practice and become better, but it would appear to me that since after all these months of practice you've made no more headway, maybe music isn't really your thing."

He acted relieved and said, "You mean not everyone can play a musical instrument?"

I said, "Well, I think everyone who is slightly intelligent can learn to push the right button on the saxophone or push down the right key on the piano according to a little black note on the sheet, but not everybody has a musical gift. It came to Beethoven differently from that." Sometimes friends can tell us things we don't see.

There are other ways to get objective counsel. You can take tests that tell you what your aptitudes are. You take SATs or ACTs and learn from those where your strengths lie. With school counselors and teachers you can go over these test results and get an idea what you are cut out to be. Most people do better in one thing than another. A young person who has real aptitude for math and quantifiable kinds of information may well need to follow this direction for life. On the other hand, if a person's skills tend to be more toward the arts and music, then perhaps the sciences aren't the best place for that person. You can learn a lot about God's will if you live your life according to the way God put you together.

Finally, Mueller said you should get moving. You should not be immobilized by your lack of certitude. Just because you don't know what you should do, you must not just sit around and wait for the bedpost to light up or writing to appear in the sky. Begin to move through life, trying to be as obedient as you know how through what God has shown you. Then he is obligated to bring to your attention those circumstances and opportunities that you might be able to use to better serve him.

In other words, the first step in planning the rest of your life and having a God-pleasing future is to make God a central part of your life, walk with Jesus Christ on a moment-by-moment basis and attempt to be obedient to Christ in that daily walk. Live a life that is moral and upright and in harmony with the Word of God, and invite Christ to guide your life so that you may be in tune with him to do his will and discern the specific steps you ought to take to find the very center of his will.

Sometimes when people talk like this, a secret fear comes to the surface. We live in a modern world, and talk about God's will sounds a bit fanatical, especially since there are so many religious nuts being given so much space in the media. We want to believe in God, but we don't want to be fanatics. This is a justifiable concern; however, it is good to keep in mind that fanaticism consists not of too much God but too little brains. If, in fact, if there is a God—and we Christians believe that there is—and if we are privileged to know of his very nature and character because Jesus Christ visited our planet, then it is impossible to take him too seriously. The Bible tells us to "test the spirits" to determine if they are of God. To be sure, the variety of religious experiences available in today's world can be confusing. All the more reason to be a part of his established church, which has guided families for generations, and to study your Bible. You've often heard of throwing out the baby with the bathwater. Many people today are too lazy to really investigate their faith, and because it is too complicated they leave God out altogether while they avoid the obvious religious charlatans.

People who don't know God, who choose to live alone and separate from him, have none of his help. We are promised in

God's Word that he will help us and that his Holy Spirit will be a friend who walks beside us with his hand on our shoulders, comforting, encouraging, instructing, and guiding us as we make decisions. For some people who are not Christians, who don't know God, the future may be a very frightening thing. The whole future looks like a swamp of some kind. They feel like they are on Swiss cheese ready to fall through a hole at any minute. We know, however, that God made the world and us, and the future is in his hands. He is the Alpha and Omega, the beginning and the end, and we can trust him totally and completely. He is a God of love who cares for us. He would never lead us into something that would be wrong for us, but he wants us to be exactly in the place right for us. With this loving care he nudges us and lures us toward those things that can be most beneficial for our lives and future.

We can trust God to open doors for us and to close them, too. We keep moving through these open doors, but when a door is shut, we test it to see if we can open it. If not, we accept that this is his will for us and we seek an alternate route through this maze of life. The promise that God gives to us as Christians is that we don't have to live this life alone. Amazingly, some people who are Christians live as though there is no God. They skip this step and try to do everything in their own strength. They don't come to him with their problems in prayer or ask for guidance in daily decisions. They do not turn their future over to him and ask him to make crooked places straight. They live, as it were, as if they were practical atheists. This is unnecessary. Life does not have to be nearly so fearful as long as we know that God goes before us as our captain, behind us as the rear guard of our salvation, under us with his mighty arms, and over us with his everlasting wings. All of these are poetic phrases used in the Bible to help us see that we are secure in him and that he indeed cares for us in this life and throughout all eternity.

If you go back to the beginning, you know you are a creation of God. He made you just as you are. Your height, width, color of hair, eyes, mental abilities, special gifts, and character traits come to you from God. Ultimately, criticism of yourself and what you are is criticism of the Creator. When you accept who you are and realize God made you just for this purpose, then your task is to find the purpose for which God brought you into the world. Why did he want someone of your exact height, weight, makeup? What is the spot that he perfectly made for you to fill in today's needs?

Today we study ecology. Most students are aware of the ecosystems and how very intricately God has put the world together, how every microorganism as well as every plant and every animal fills its spot in the ecological balance and structure. Isn't it strange to live life as if the most outstanding part of God's creation—humankind—would be the one thing that doesn't fit in and doesn't make sense, that God would make creatures to stick out like sore thumbs without a place in his creation? Viewing the rest of the world and how well God has made it makes that thought absurd. Obviously if God made humans his primary and supreme creation, then he had a desire for each of our lives to fit in. Our task is to yield ourselves to him and allow him to guide us, over time and through experiences as we seek him wholeheartedly, to the right things.

When I was a college student, I chose two Bible verses to be the centerpiece of my life. Matthew 6:33 says, "Seek first the kingdom of God and His righteousness, and all these things shall be added to you." The other verse is Proverbs 3:5–6, "Trust in the LORD with all your heart, and lean not on your own understanding; in all your ways acknowledge Him, and He shall direct your paths." By putting God first, seeking him above all other things, and then trusting him with all your heart, you may be sure your life will be guided according to his paths. I would have to say after all these many years that God has never let me down nor disappointed me. He has always taken care of me, and because of this I desire that you as a recent graduate may do the same thing. If you do, these promises are as sure as the law of gravity. Just as surely as when you drop your keys off your key ring and they fall to the floor rather than go to the ceiling, you can trust that God will take care of you if you put him first and if you trust him with all your heart and allow him to be the controlling factor in your daily living.

Where God will be in your life and your future is the first important decision, the first great choice you make in forming the future of your adult life. It's a bit awe inspiring and frightening to think that there are people who, when they move into this adult phase, when they have their independence, exercise the independence in rebellion and choose to live separate from God. It's no wonder to us that the world is in its present condition and people have the problems they do when we see so many living their lives totally separate from God and not putting this important first building stone into the building of their future. Make sure God has his proper place in the planning of your future decisions.

As I discussed this chapter with students, they gave several suggestions that you may find helpful.

> "Don't be afraid of the why questions. Most people you meet are all wrapped up in the what and the how or the how much. Really, these don't make any sense without the why. God gives us a reason for our existence and an idea of where we fit in. If I didn't have my faith, I'd probably live

just like the others who are on their own. Because I know Christ, I have purpose. Sure, I want to be professionally competent and want to get ahead, but mostly I want to participate with God in his purpose for creating the world and me. I want to make a contribution. If you don't know why you are here, then what you do doesn't make much difference."

"When it comes right down to it, I'm really on my own right now and could fool my parents about my Christian walk, but I've found out on a practical basis that if I discipline myself and don't neglect my prayer life and devotional time, my life goes better. It's that simple. Life works better with God involved. He doesn't force himself on us. We have to make time to make room for him."

"Get involved in a church. Don't just say, 'I still pray.' A church can be like a family when you are away from home. Just going to a different church every week doesn't do it. You have to commit yourself to one church and be a part of it. Then it really pays off."

Being Yourself

As I have said, criticism of ourselves is ultimately criticism of God, because as David the psalmist wrote, "It is He who has made us, and not we ourselves" (Ps. 100:3). Coming to terms with what we can change in ourselves and what we can't is one of life's most important lessons. Obviously we can change our hairstyle, take medication to clear up complexion problems, brush our teeth, use deodorant, visit an orthodontist, or get contact lenses. There is nothing wrong with being in style or attempting to make ourselves as attractive as possible.

There are, however, many things we really cannot adjust, which for reasons of his own God has built into each of us. Our

"Sometimes I watch people 'playing the role' and I feel like I could throw up. Other times I want to tell them to relax and not try so hard. If they would be themselves, others would like them for who they are. The problem is I do the same thing but in different ways. I'm especially this way around people I want to impress. I talk too much, I brag, sometimes I exaggerate. I've decided that more or less everybody does this, but when I meet someone who is relaxed and genuine, I feel jealous and wonder how they do it."

height, basic body type, facial features, and even certain characteristics of temperament are beyond our control. Part of a Christian's faith is the belief that God knew exactly what he was doing when he made each of us. For some reason God determined that there was a special reason for someone like each of us to be created, and in fact, if we were not here, the world would miss some specific uniqueness that is each of us. No two people are exactly alike and for good reason. God has built variety into the human experience, and we are a part of the mosaic that makes up the whole. Rather than think of ourselves as wanting to conform to the image of another person, we must learn to celebrate the fact that we are unique creations of the holy God.

When people are young and immature, they often admire a person who achieves some kind of success. They want to fit in and be accepted, so they try to imitate that person's clothes, looks, or behavior and thereby live in his or her reflected glow. In reality, the imitators lose their own personalities and charm and really never get the other person's either. The resulting feeling of emptiness and lack of fulfillment is often then turned into a feeling of rejection, when in reality what has been rejected is the fake or imitation self.

One of the neat things about maturing and getting out of the high school atmosphere is that people of college age are beginning to grow out of the fantasy world that promises a visit from the good fairy to turn them into someone of their own imagination. With the growing out of this fantasy is the more mature attitude of accepting themselves and others for who they are. They can begin to celebrate diversity of various types. They realize that the physical attributes of people are not the most important characteristics, that qualities of character and personality are actually of greater substance. They begin to value people for their loyalty, insight, sensitivity, compassion, drive, and desire to serve and contribute, as well as for such obvious things as beauty, athletic ability, or popularity.

God has given each of us gifts that are unique to us and that are for the enrichment and enjoyment of those around us. Part of the challenge is to believe this by faith and then to develop our strengths for our own happiness and for the good of others.

Everyone has seen an overhead projector. Think of yourself this way. Suppose each person you know, including yourself, could be diagrammed like the schematic drawing on the back of your TV set that describes the complex wiring. Now, people are infinitely more complex than mere TV sets, but just for fun imagine that all of the intricacies that make up a human being could be reduced to a diagram on a transparency and then projected on a screen.

If everyone you know, indeed everyone in the world, had their own transparency and each exactly to scale, you could stack them on top of each other and shine the light of the overhead projector through them all. In each case, including yours, something unique would stand out from all of the others. This is your uniqueness that God built into you. If you do not allow that genuine uniqueness to be developed, then all of the rest of us will be impoverished to the degree that we were robbed of what God gave the world when he made you. One of your tasks for these next years is to explore all of the options and possibilities, to find those things that you are best suited for and allow yourself to shine through your special uniqueness. For some people this can be a very difficult challenge because of perceived or real deficiencies, but all have some special ability.

Doubtless you have heard of Helen Keller who, though blind and deaf, overcame her difficulties and contributed to all who knew or even heard of her. Few are asked to overcome such great obstacles, yet many are defeated by imagined shortcomings or surface things such as weight, complexion, protruding ears, or other equally inconsequential things, unable to overcome them as a source of feeling depressed. Remember that you are special because you were God's idea and got your start in his mind. Regardless of the color of your skin, your physical beauty, athletic ability, family background, academic prowess, height, weight, or anything else, remember that God loves you and will never reject you. You can always count on that. He says in the Bible that he is a friend that sticks closer than a brother and that he will never leave you nor forsake you.

Self-esteem starts with the immovable fact that you are loved by God. Accept the major premise that if he made you he must have known what he was doing. If so, all you have to do is discover how you can best fit in and make your contribution to this world. It's good to have childhood and high school in the past, because so many things there revolve around surface things like good looks and popularity, cliques and conformity. Now you are entering the more mature stage of your life when you can be the real you and enjoy what God had in mind when he first created you.

4

Why College?

The complexity of modern culture makes the postponement of marriage a common thing in today's world. These complexities require that young people be better prepared before they enter adulthood than they ever needed to be in former generations. I'd like to mention three things that I believe can be accomplished by going to college that are very important during these preparation years. Let me acknowledge at the onset that not everyone does go to college, and indeed perhaps not everyone should go to college; however, the arguments for going far outweigh those against it. If a young person today decides to immediately enter the workplace, regardless of where he or she enters, eventually to rise

"Every kid in my class wondered why they call it 'commencement.' It ought to be called the finish or something like that. I just couldn't wait to get out of high school and not have homework anymore. College seemed like such a long time. Four more years of classes, studies, books, libraries, and junk like that, but now that I'm in college, I realize that though it is something like high school, it is really different. After I went home on my first vacation and talked to my high school friends, I can see the reason. Our worlds are really growing apart. I thought we were best friends and had a lot in common. Now I realize that this was pretty superficial. Their world seems to be actually shrinking, while mine is growing. They are becoming so set in their ways, and in many ways I'm less sure of myself. I just know that I'm on the right track, and if I never make more money or become financially successful, I still feel I'm becoming a different person. College stretches you, and you just don't fit in the old crowd any more. I see now that I'm beginning to understand the possibilities that my life holds for me, and it is exciting. I love it!"

above the very bottom floor of employment opportunities and economic standards it will be necessary to get some form of additional education, either through training by industry or by a community based vocational training center. Only the most menial jobs paying the very minimum wages will be available to those who do not seek education beyond high school. I would not list vocational preparation first in my reasons for considering college. I know that many parents are concerned about "marketable skills," and these are important. What you are, however, is far more important than what you do.

My first reason for attending college and the one I would strongly urge you to consider is closely connected to the previous chapter about doing God's will and developing your personal autonomy. A frequently heard commercial for the United States Army says, "Be all that you can be in the Army," and for some people this may be a way to get further education and be lifted out of a dead-end corner. Regardless of the truthfulness of that message, let me say that it is important that everyone be all that they can be. Being is more basic than doing or having. It is about your very nature and essence.

Ultimately college is not about vocational preparation but at its core is about being or becoming. It is about developing one's person intellectually and socially so as to be what God intended and to make the greatest contribution within God's purposes for his world. Perhaps the greatest compliment you can give to any friend is to want to know more about that person. If God is your friend, then you will want to know all that you can about him and the world he has created. Someone has said that education is really the business of thinking God's thoughts after him. That means to understand the physical world that God has created with all of its complexity and interrelatedness, to understand God's work in human history, through the great events of history, to see the accomplishments of humankind and the mistakes and successes that have formed the culture to this point in time. Education is to study the great concepts that God has put in the minds of people through great literature and philosophy. It is to be familiar with the beauty that he has written into his universe in the form of art and music. It is to see how people affect nature and vice versa, and how in various historic and political configurations people have learned to relate to one another.

As you grow in your understandings of these various disciplines, you become more of what you can be and are able to give of your best to the Master rather than settle for mediocrity. As you fulfill the largest potential that God has built into you, you glorify him. This cannot be done without effort and is very difficult to do alone. I would not argue that it is impossible to gain an education without going to college. People can read, and there is a great deal available for self-improvement in modern life. People can expose themselves to much of the world through communications media and travel. Many people are self-taught. However, self-education is demanding and expensive and usually difficult to do with life's competing demands. When you enter a program specifically geared to accomplish this purpose, you can do it better. Colleges are set up for that purpose. You do it better in interaction with other learners of your own age as well as under the care and tutelage of professors who have spent a great deal of time and energy and money to prepare themselves to make these great contributions to your life. In no place in modern culture is there more access to the totality of human experience and understanding than in the college.

The second reason that I believe it is important to pursue a college education is that during your college years you will begin to integrate the various bits of information you have collected over your younger years and put them into some sort of a picture that makes sense to you. We call this a synoptic view or worldview. It is a way of looking at the world by having an overall understanding of how the world was made, for what purpose, and how everyone fits into it. Most people form their worldviews during college age. Whether a worldview is inadequate or complete, whether it is Christian or self-centered, whether it is contributive or parasitical is determined largely by how it is put together and under what influence.

I would argue not only for college but for a Christian college, especially in regard to this second aspect of college education—the development of a worldview. Christians see God as the unifying influence and force in the universe, and it is during the college years that young Christians begin to fit together the varying pieces of the picture of God's creative effort and its purposes, including their purpose for being on the earth.

College will give you an opportunity to be exposed to ideas, lifestyles, cultures, languages, thoughts, and expressions of various peoples without having to buy a plane ticket and spending extended time in each place getting face-to-face information. College education will expand your vision beyond the borders of your own community. It will help you to escape what some call the "cage of smallness" that circumscribes many people's lives. Before I went to college, I had never attended a symphony orchestra concert. In fact, I didn't think it was very cool to do so because none of my high school friends did anything like it. When I arrived at college as a freshman, there was a program of big brothers and sisters. The big brother assigned to me turned out to be the student body president. I hadn't known that at the time I was given his name and had no idea what to expect when I met him. I found, however, that he was a senior who was a very good student, was extremely manly, polite, and had all the characteristics that I had looked up to all of my life. When he suggested we do something together, it was that we attend the local symphony concert on a Saturday evening. I was too young and intimidated to say no, and so we went. He explained to me what was happening, something about the music, told me what to listen for and how to appreciate it. Suddenly my world had grown larger than it had been up until that time. As I write these words, I am listening to music that I never would have appreciated unless I had had this exposure.

In college you are exposed to all sorts of things that you've never experienced before, and each time you grow a little more. Your view of the world grows until you have developed the ability to enjoy and understand the world to a greater degree than you could have possibly done without this experience.

It's only last that I list vocational preparation as the reason to consider college. The truth of the matter is that right now a college graduate on average earns $1200 a month more than a noncollege graduate. This is a national average. It means that the typical male college graduate will earn something in the neighborhood of $350–500,000 more in his lifetime than will a person who graduates from high school only.

This speaks, of course, of financial remuneration. The other side of this is that generally speaking, college students get to do the kind of work they want to do rather than what is available or what is forced on them. They have freedom to a much greater degree. There are many men and women who have worked an entire lifetime at a job that they hate. How much better to explore the possibilities, think through what kinds of vocations are available, and then go about the business of preparing for that particular career and spend your lifetime doing something you like while being paid a great deal more to do it. It simply makes sense.

The sad truth is that without this kind of preparation there are not going to be jobs for a great portion of the population except at the very lowest levels that pay the very least money. Even in today's factories the robotic equipment requires a higher level of specialization than was once needed in assembly-line factories.

The highest paying jobs in factories in the day of your grandfather were jobs such as welding. Today welding is almost exclusively done by robots and machines. The person who controls and understands the robot has a great deal of different information and education from the person who used to do the welding by hand. People have been replaced by machines, and unless people are capable of controlling and understanding the machines, they will be obsolete.

I meet many young people who think they are going to be the exception to the rule. Some think they can make it big in rock music. They read all the magazines about gold and platinum records and believe that somehow they can compete musically or be more outrageous than some other group. Certainly some have succeeded; however, as is the case with professional sports, it is a long shot at best. I've met many young men who were the greatest in their neighborhood in basketball. They were high school stars and were sure that all they had to do was go somewhere and play basketball until they were discovered by the NBA. Unfortunately this seldom happens. The nearest town to where I live has a population of about 30,000 people. In the entire history of that city not a single one of all the high school baseball players has ever made it to the major leagues, and the one basketball player who got a shot at the professional ranks was sent down to the minor leagues and is unable to make the grade. He dropped out of college and so is stuck with only one option—basketball. I hope he makes it, but he is growing older and keeps getting passed over. A contemporary of his in a neighboring high school finished his college degree, tried it in the NBA, couldn't quite make it, and is now a coach and moving along in his career.

Probably every high school student has noticed the graduates of ten years ago who return to watch the high school games in their worn-out letter jackets and wondered why these people have not progressed beyond their one time in the sun. There is absolutely nothing wrong with being proud of your high school accomplishments, but it is very important that you grow as a person and learn how to continue growing so that you do not get stuck looking through the rearview mirror of life from graduation on. If at all possible, and usually it is, I would encourage you to take advantage of the educational opportunities provided by this society and give yourself time for the preparation of the rest of your life.

5

What Kind of College?

olleges come in all sizes and shapes. In fact, this is one of the distinguishing characteristics of American higher education and one of its greatest strengths. Actually there are about 3500 colleges and universities in the United States. Some are very small and specific in their offerings and may have as few as one hundred or so students. Other multi-universities, as they are sometimes called, have tens of thousands of students.

Most high school students are familiar with the state universities in their area. In fact, the personal identity of many people is tied to the win-loss records of their sports teams. I live in Indiana, and though sometimes we blush a little at the publicity

"At our high school it was pretty well divided as to college or not—about half-and-half. Most of the class had pretty well made up their mind based on where their friends had gone or where the action was relating to parties and the wild life. We discussed various options, but mostly it boiled down to friends and money. I had a little more background because my sister and her friends had gone to college, and so I had a better idea. But it's really confusing because it sort of breaks up the old gang. They go away to different places, and it's kind of sad in a way. I feel I made a good choice, but I think it was because my sister did."

that often surrounds Bobby Knight, we all are proud of Indiana University basketball. Thousands of people in our state wear IU sweatshirts and have IU bumper stickers on their automobiles, even though they have never attended a class at the university. Somehow they feel by wearing the colors they can share the glow of basketball victories and make living in a rural midwestern state more prestigious. They tire of hearing people talk about New York and California and want to say to all who look at them, "Hey! We're important, too! We have a great basketball team!" And most times they are right.

There is nothing wrong with regional pride nor deeply distressing about borrowing identity from someone else. When you choose a college, however, it is important to weigh other factors as you make your decision.

The state colleges and universities are in many ways our national pride. They have been built and are supported by the taxes of citizens to insure that all worthy young people have a chance to get a college education if they truly want one. Most states have built junior colleges or community colleges to take the overflow of those who are unable to afford to go away from home to a resident campus, or to provide a way for students who did not do as well in high school as they might have to prove themselves and to obtain remedial help. These schools are academically solid for the most part but lack some of the frills and glamour of the main campuses. In most cases you can transfer credit from one to the other and even get a degree through the combined institutions. No country in the world makes education more accessible to a greater number of its citizens.

In addition to these schools with which most people are familiar are hundreds of private colleges and universities which are not supported by tax money but attempt to make it possible for students of all economic backgrounds to attend. Many of these private schools, in fact most of them, were first supported by churches—Catholic, Protestant and Jewish—to provide education for their members and to instruct the students on the specific and unique beliefs of the sponsoring groups.

Most of the oldest of these schools, now called the Ivy League schools, were of this type and first existed to prepare men for the ministry. They were built on what we call the American colonial model—about five hundred students and faculty living in a community was considered to be nearly ideal. Most are larger now and provide resources that smaller schools usually cannot afford, especially in science, engineering, and high tech computer-oriented areas.

Many of the schools that were church supported have become independent of the control of the churches, although some maintain loose historic affiliations while they seek broader secular support. Private schools can do things their own way without government interference. This allows for diversity within our educational system. Most of the private schools are accredited by the same associations that accredit the larger universities.

Besides some being private and some state-supported schools, there are other differences. Most small colleges and universities put greater emphasis on teaching undergraduates—students seeking bachelor's degrees—than on graduate programs—older students seeking a master's degree or doctorate. Many private colleges and universities have graduate programs, but for right now we won't go into that aspect of it. It is important, however, to go to a respected school for your undergraduate degree if you plan to go on to further graduate education. Because many private colleges are more selective (meaning you have to have better grades to be accepted) and because they usually have smaller classes for underclassmen (freshmen and sophomores), they provide a good solid foundation for graduate school. In small colleges the student-faculty ratio is usually about fifteen or twenty to one. In large state schools it is not uncommon to attend classes with two hundred or three hundred other students. Obviously you can get more help and be more deeply involved with your professors in the smaller classes.

In addition, in most cases at large state institutions undergraduates are taught by teaching assistants—students who have finished their undergraduate degrees and are working with the professors on their advanced degrees (master's or doctorate). They are provided scholarships and stipends to pay for their education for teaching undergraduates. Many of them are enthusiastic and well-prepared. However, in smaller schools you are usually taught by professors who already have advanced degrees and who believe that teaching is their calling. They do some research, usually tied to the subject they teach, but their delight is in igniting the interest of their students in their subject. (In the institution where I work, 70 percent of all the teachers have a doctoral degree or its equivalent in their particular fields.)

When you are making your college choice, you want to be aware of some of these differences. Smaller, private colleges may sometimes be harder to get into and may cost more money but are often solid options, especially if you seek personal attention and are able to compete. Most will be forthright with you and not accept you unless they are confident of your ability to succeed.

It is not the end of the world if you get turned down. I often encourage "late bloomers," or students without the necessary test scores, to establish themselves in a less selective college and then when they have proved that they can do college work to transfer to the college of their choice. It is almost always easier to transfer into a selective school than to gain initial acceptance. I've watched many do it this way and have rejoiced with them at their success.

When all the dust has settled, the real question has to do with studies and academic offerings. Make sure that you read the school's catalog and that it offers majors in your area of interest. (We'll talk about that later, lest you think you have to have it all decided before you go to college. The largest major at most colleges among underclassmen is "undeclared," and the second largest is "undecided.")

In addition to the private-public option is the matter of campus atmosphere and student life to consider. Most schools provide special weekends or visitation days so prospective students can get a feel of what the place is like. Not every school is right for everyone. It is important to feel that you "fit." If possible visit several schools and spend as much time as you can. Ask questions, especially of students to see what they think. Is the campus really like the viewbook says it is? Do professors have time to talk to you? Do academic advisors care about students' specific needs? What is the social life like? And if you are a Christian, what is the school's attitude toward people who have convictions? Are they tolerant of various views? What if you don't have a lot of money? Can you still be accepted? These and other questions that you think of will help you know if this is the place for you.

These are not the only considerations nor the only options. Not all people feel a bent toward study or academics. Some have high levels of interest in art, music, mechanics, business, agriculture, landscaping, and many other specific areas. Though I would argue that ideally a broad-based, liberal arts education would be good for everyone, not all agree nor are all interested. Some feel quite focused and for personal reasons, including economic realities, want to enter a career or the workplace as quickly as possible. There are business colleges, vocational colleges, and dozens of other public and private schools, institutes, and conservatories to meet these interests. I would encourage you to get the best possible preparation so that you can achieve your goals, contribute to your world, and be as personally fulfilled as possible. Don't shortchange yourself and spend a lifetime regretting it.

Generally speaking, you will not rise above the breadth of your preparation. Remember in geometry when you learned to draw an equilateral triangle with a compass? That's what I'm trying to say. The height of your accomplishment will generally be the length of your base. The broader your background, the better.

Students discussing college choices made the following interesting suggestions.

"Don't go as far away from home as possible. Sometimes when you are at home in high school you feel restricted and think, 'Just wait until I go away to college. I'll go as far as possible so nobody can check up on me.' This is really not very smart and not financially realistic, either. Convenience in getting home for vacations and visits is very important. Eight or ten hours of driving will get you to most good options."

"If you are a Christian and choose a state school, be sure to get involved right away with a church or Christian campus group like InterVarsity Christian Fellowship, Campus Crusade for Christ, or one of the denominational groups. The wild life is very seductive, and you can get in over your head before you realize it."

"I went to a state school, and it's not so much the fear of losing your faith as it is getting an education built on a totally relational or secular base and kind of wasting your time. As a Christian you can be very lonely unless you really look for Christian friends. Eventually I met several, but if I had not made an effort I would have had no social life other than the party crowd."

"I think it is largely a matter of what you really want. If you are trying to lead two lives and deceive your parents, you can go to a Christian college and use it as a cover-up to live a very wild life. When you get to college, wherever you go, you have to decide what kind of person you want to be and what you really want to get out of it. You've got to decide if you want academics, success, power, money, or a certain lifestyle. You've got to decide what you want."

"I have high school friends who didn't go to college or any local school and already are bored and into drugs and alcohol like you wouldn't believe. I think they do this to try to escape a bad decision or to cover up a bad attitude. I wish some of them would not be so stubborn and change their minds before they get locked in and can't really do anything about it."

"I started at another college and transferred after I had a better idea of what I wanted. I think for me this was a good idea. Now I feel like I've always been here."

"My folks didn't want me at a Christian college because they thought that a state school had more prestige. Now they are glad for me because they've seen what has happened to some of my friends who got caught up in the wrong things."

The Christian College Option

I am devoting this chapter to the Christian college because I will strongly argue that if you are a serious Christian, you should give special attention to this particular decision.

When I say Christian college, I speak of a whole range of colleges and smaller universities that attempt to integrate faith and learning. These schools are built on several specific premises. They believe that this is a created world. They may differ in their approaches to the methodology (that is, how God created the world), and they may hold various views about how long it took God to do it (from six twenty-four-hour days to perhaps millions of years), but they all are uniquely distinguished from their sec-

> *"All through high school I struggled with the fact that there were so few Christians in my classes. We were always a minority and had to really fight for our convictions in many of our classes. Eventually it became a losing proposition because of the prejudice of teachers, so I just kept my mouth shut and did my best to meet their expectations. I really couldn't wait to go to a Christian college where I could explore my faith along with my studies. I also got tired of the constant hassle over listening to sewer-mouthed people. I don't feel even slightly sorry I am at a Christian college. We have more fun, I think, because we are not living deceptive lives. I can do anything I want, but I really want to know God better and live for him."*

ular counterparts in that they insist that all faculty believe in God and that the world is his creative accomplishment.

Although some are supported and controlled by specific denominations, some are interdenominational, and all may have slightly different doctrinal statements, all would agree to the historic affirmation of faith as expressed in the Apostle's Creed. You have probably said it in church: "I believe in God the Father Almighty, maker of heaven and earth, and in Jesus Christ, his only Son, our Lord, who was conceived by the Holy Spirit, born of the virgin Mary, suffered under Pontius Pilate, was crucified, dead, and buried. The third day he rose from the dead. He ascended into heaven and sits at the right hand of God the Father; from thence he shall come to judge the living and the dead. I believe in the Holy Spirit, the holy catholic church, the communion of saints, the forgiveness of sins, the resurrection of the body, and the life everlasting. Amen."

These schools further take the Bible seriously and affirm its authority as God's revelation of himself to humankind. Though there is quite a bit of diversity among these schools, and each has its own unique history and personality, they are "sister" institutions and may in some ways be viewed as a kind of decentralized national Christian university of 100,000 or more students.

Taylor University, where I serve, is a part of a group of colleges called the Christian College Consortium. (A list of these schools may be found in the back of this book.) There are, of course, many more denominational Christian colleges in the country which are not members but are built upon similar principles. You might find it helpful to consult your pastor or youth director about schools that they would recommend.

Two arguments against going to a Christian college are often put to me by both students and parents. The first is that it is possible to go to a secular institution and still keep one's faith intact. I agree with this and, in fact, would say that this is more possible today than it was in my youth. There are many vital and effective evangelical ministries on secular campuses today such as Campus Crusade for Christ and InterVarsity Christian Fellowship, as well as denominational outreaches and fellowship groups. My argument would be that you can keep the faith by staying at home. The intention of education is to grow as a person in a holistic manner: intellectually, spiritually, physically, socially, and in one's sense of purpose and meaning. If the professors teaching you were neutral as to their belief systems, then you would be free to grow on your own; however, your college experience in the classroom would not contribute either positively or negatively to your spiritual growth.

In the real world, however, professors are not values neutral. Many are openly hostile to the Christian gospel and sometimes hostile toward the Christian student for a variety of reasons. Some do not understand the Christian message and operate from unfortunate or uninformed stereotypes—even caricatures—of the gospel. Others have had harmful and negative personal experiences with Christians, and some have deep and well-formed intellectual reservations about the nature of Christian revelation and truth. Many, if not most, would argue that it is impossible to be both Christian and intellectually respectable, because there are no absolutes and all truth is relative.

Christians disagree with this because of their faith in God. Christians believe that God exists, is an absolute, and has spoken with certainty through the Bible, his Son, and the created order. This is a basic disagreement between secular and Christian scholars. The best of both try to be civil and open to each other's views; however, at the foundation they agree to disagree about their presuppositions. None are able to totally hide their bias from their students and, in fact, do influence them by the power of their intellect and the quality of their lifestyles. Professors are very important, because education is not merely the transfer of information. Education is interactive, and your professors' viewpoints will come through over time.

During this particular period of history we are making progress on overcoming our prejudices and are striving for understanding among diverse peoples. Educated and cultured people do not use racial or ethnic jokes or slurs. Fair and informed people do not discriminate against others because of gender, nationality, color, education, or physical or mental differences. The only group that can be attacked without fear of rebuttal in our current culture is evangelical Christians. This will doubtless pass with time, but at present, communications media and academia are not free of hostility, bias, and intolerance. I contend that a Christian college is a good choice because during your formative years, as you are getting your own worldview put together, it is desirable to be taught by fair-minded, well-prepared Christian professors.

The second argument that I often hear is that all of us have to meet secular arguments and hostility sooner or later and that a Christian college is too protected an environment to prepare people for the "real world." Doubtless there are examples of Christian colleges or certain teachers who have indeed approached learning in this way and actually indoctrinated rather than educated. By indoctrination I speak of the process of simply transferring unexamined dogma from the teacher to the student without honest, critical examination or opportunity for open discussion or disagreement. There is a place for indoctrination, such as in training soldiers how to clean a rifle or maintain a uniform. There is no place for this in education, and good Christian professors are aware of this.

They are careful to present opposing views fairly and often invite spokespersons of other views to present them to their students. They assign reading in diverse literature and attempt to present all sides of issues. I would argue that they do as good and often a much better job than many secular professors do with Christian or even traditional and classical thought. Students are influenced by professors; otherwise, why have them? We might as well give in to using teaching machines exclusively and thus cut down the cost of education if we believe professors have no influence. Using this method you could trust all the students in America with one professor in each discipline and the proper level of television availability. It is precisely the diversity, personality, inspiration, interaction, mentoring, and commitment of professors that makes a good learning environment.

Students like you living in the modern world are not naive and isolated. If you live in a small town in a sparsely populated state, you are exposed to the same cultural input as those in major cities and sometimes have had more exposure for reasons of economics and initiative. The communications media have made our world a global village. Students in Syria and Kenya watch Michael Jackson.

Today's students are not ignorant of the varieties in other cultures. You may not be a whiz at locating the capitals of small African countries, but you are not as isolated from the challenges of diversity—from race to drugs to language to sexuality—as were your grandparents. Most Christian colleges were involved with internationalism long before their secular counterparts. Decades before international trade in the Pacific rim was a subject in daily news broadcasts, Christian missionaries were actually living in those countries, learning the languages, educating, and healing. They were respecting other cultures and bringing information and culture back to the United States.

All of the Christian colleges have international students who not only attend classes but live in the residence halls, eat meals at the same tables, and enter into the daily life of students on the campus. On most large secular campuses the international students are often isolated and uninvolved except in the classroom and in official efforts by administrators to maintain multicultural diversity. This is true of other diversities as well. But on the small campus there is often a family atmosphere that insists on involvement of all of the members.

Most Christian colleges have chapel services on a regular basis that enable the entire learning community to relate spiritual experiences. This is impossible in a giant multi-university.

I will not try to argue that there is no need for our large state research institutions. They are, in fact, a source of deserved pride worldwide. As you grow and develop you may decide to pursue graduate education. By that time you will have become a self-regulating young adult with a developed worldview. You will be able to build on a solid Christian foundation without being unduly intimidated by diversity and even some hostility.

As you make your college decision, be sure that you explore the option of the Christian college. Students' satisfaction is one of the best indicators of schools providing what students really want. The retention rate at the top Christian schools is 85–95 percent. (That is how many students eligible to return each year actually do.) The national percentage hovers between 50 and 60 percent. This certainly says something about how students feel, and after all, they are the people for whom colleges exist.

7

Let's Party!

Almost all healthy people like to have a good time. I'm sure Jesus and his disciples did some clowning around and horseplay. Young men traveling together and sharing meals and experiences always have and always will. We know that they went fishing and had picnics, attended parties and weddings. They doubtless drank wine; however, we never read that any of them became drunk or abusive, nor do we know of sexual looseness. They had women friends, some of whom were, without doubt, girlfriends. They followed sports and knew of the discipline of athletic training. They sat around campfires and talked. Sometimes they had

> *"The alcohol-and-sex scene at my high school was overwhelming. Many of my friends lived to party every weekend and sometimes during the week. When you are a freshman or sophomore you really think this is cool, but for me, at least, it became so predictable. Who wants to spend every weekend with a headache or cleaning up crying and puking friends? You wouldn't believe it if I told you all of the stuff that happened. Some like it and want four more years of it, but I would prefer a good time without the disgusting immaturity. Not everyone in high school lived this way, and I didn't want to in college, but I still wanted to have a good time. In college you can be your own person more easily. I like that."*

what college students call bull sessions, and sometimes they argued and disagreed.

Actually they were in what today's educators call a classroom without walls. Jesus was their professor and interacted with them through lectures, examples, stories, experiences, and questions. He never discouraged their ordinary lives and diversions. College-age young people enjoy these same opportunities, and I am confident that God smiles at these activities as Jesus did with his disciples.

My wife, Janie, and I were on a large state university campus recently on the day the freshmen arrived. We watched them walk down the streets between the fraternity and sorority houses trying ever so hard to look cool and unafraid. Sophomores and upperclass students were on the porches of the houses, laughing and largely ignoring the underclassmen, intentionally hoping to intimidate them. The freshmen were wearing their new clothes, carefully selected to be "in" but not look planned.

We both smiled and remembered our own freshman days. My first college experience was exactly like theirs, though they happened several decades apart. My mind returned to fraternity smokers and Greek trade parties between our fraternity and sororities. I remembered how seductive the climate was to bawdy jokes, alcohol, and obligatory sex. We really wanted to be grown up, and now at last we were free. There were no restrictions; in fact, there was a kind of expectation that we should throw off the restraints of our families and be worldly-wise. Actually I had not seen many of my high school friends drunk. Sometimes they would get silly and sometimes they would vomit, but I never saw them lose all of their inhibitions. I suppose it was because they had to go home afterward and feared being found out.

As I watched these freshmen, I wondered, would they be like we were? Would they try to act like all this was old hat and they were really sophisticated? Would they abandon their standards and convictions to fit in and be accepted? I remember that the guys in the fraternity always saw the nondrinking girls as a kind of challenge. As the drinks were passed around the room, many would say, "No, thank you," the first time or the second. On the third pass around most would take one, planning to just hold it and let it die, happy to set it down on an end table before they left or pour it down the sink or in a planter. By the fourth pass most would begin to sip, and the goal was achieved. In our day this was a prelude to breaking down inhibitions with the hope of at least heavy petting, if not actual sex.

I wondered about today. Is it different? I knew about alcohol and tobacco, but how about drugs? Does the fact that even respectable, highly paid television personalities joke about coke and marijuana have an effect on today's freshmen? Does the expectation of being sexually active as a teenager and the familiarity of the correct use of the condom change things? You and I both know it does and we also know that if parents knew how much, they would all be on Valium or follow us everywhere we went. One of the attractions of college is freedom. Basically there is nothing wrong with that, for as I've pointed out, it is an inescapable part of the maturing process.

Today's campus, however, is a kind of island in the midst of a secular society. In states where you cannot legally buy alcohol until age twenty-one, you can drink without restraint in college connected apartments and fraternity houses. In fact, you are expected to, and the authorities, quite unlike Jesus with his constant reminders to his students about moral responsibility, wink at this behavior or in some cases feel it is necessary so students can become independent and develop their own autonomy. Many professors, especially graduate assistants, are very young and have not yet resolved their own conflicts with their own parents. They are often mature in their academic discipline and undeniably bright intellectually but struggle with their own independence and are in a state of reaction against authority—especially conventional culture, the church, and their parents.

You've probably seen this with young teachers in high school. One of my daughters came home from high school disturbed by a situation in one of her classes. She was somewhat exasperated by a very young and energetic social-science teacher. He was one of her favorites because he was smart and very skilled at classroom interaction. He exposed the students to challenging new ideas and was genuinely interested in them on a personal level. He gave them a questionnaire with a long list of value statements like, "It is acceptable to get drunk once in a while, especially if you have been under great pressure," or "Sex is not wrong outside of marriage if you both truly love each other and take proper precautions." The students were supposed to say first whether their parents or guardians would agree with each statement and then express their own preference. The purpose of this exercise was to determine to what degree the students agreed with their parents or authority figure. The questionnaires were coded to protect the identities of the students, yet each knew his or her own number.

The next day the teacher discussed the answers and indicated that it was, in his opinion, healthy to disagree with parents on these issues because times were changing and society was no longer bound by certain mores and folkways of the past. He then held up one of the papers, and to my daughter's amazement she recognized her number, hoping that no one else knew it. He announced to the class that here was a very sick young person psychologically, because this student agreed with the parents on almost all of the issues. He explained that this student did not know how to think independently and was in for real trouble later in life because of repression of personal opinions.

My daughter recounted the incident at the supper table that evening with some level of anger and embarrassment. I asked her, "Do you think the teacher is right? Have you been beaten down by our opinions and not allowed to think for yourself? Do you feel boxed in by us and repressed?"

She began to laugh and said, "He doesn't know anything about our family! In fact, we talk openly about everything, and you never put us down. He's on the wrong track!"

I then asked her, "What do you make of this?"

She answered, "Well, I don't know, but what I think is that Mr. 'Smith' probably has problems with his parents and has not come to terms with that. He is generalizing from his own experience and feels more secure if everyone is as mad at their parents as he is with his. What do you think?"

I said, "I think you are probably pretty close to right, but in spite of this, he is a pretty good teacher, isn't he?" We laughed and agreed that all people, including teachers, have a few blind spots.

College professors have some, too, and you have to be on the alert, both socially and intellectually, not to allow their superior education, intelligence, and, more often, seeming sophistication to cause you to abandon values that existed long before your professors were born. College is a time when you learn to draw your own moral boundaries. Somewhere deep within every human being there is a line, back of which he or she will not go. It describes a person's character. As an almost illiterate friend of mine said so graphically one day, "You are what you are when you're alone in the dark." To some degree until now this line has reflected your family's views or perhaps your church's; now it must be your own.

Once a fraternity brother said to me after offering me a drink, "Oh, I'm sorry! I forgot your church frowns on alcohol."

I answered, "I couldn't care less about that. I don't drink because I've chosen not to. I'm free to do as I want about alcohol. I choose personally not to drink. That doesn't mean I can't drink. It doesn't mean that I think I'm better than you because I don't. It doesn't mean that I think that you can't be a Christian and drink. Many Christians do. What it does mean is that as I accept you as a friend and as a person who drinks, I expect you to accept me even though I don't." We have remained friends now for over thirty-five years.

Over and over students tell me, "Tell kids to choose friends wisely. It's not just a matter of temptation; in fact, you learn not to make everything black and white. A lot of people choose different behaviors and not all are bad if they are not taken to extreme. The really important thing is that the goals, character, and integrity of your friends will rub off on you. It's important to choose friends who value the things you value. If you are committed to being a good student and your friends are always trying to tempt you to goof off and party, you will be torn and probably not get the grades you want. The same is true about loyalty and confidences. If your friends lack integrity, then you can't trust them, and your secrets will be spread everywhere. Friends should make you more what you want to be, not drag you down."

Another student put it this way: "Sometimes friendships are for the purpose of helping others. Jesus was accused of spending his time with drunkards and sinners, and he said that the healthy don't need a doctor but those who are sick do. You must be careful that you don't rationalize and that you don't get pulled under yourself. But as a Christian you are also supposed to take risks for the sake of others."

All of us must weigh our actions in light of God's Word and Jesus' example. We must also weigh the consequences of our behavior in light of our culture and the welfare of others. Freedom is a very wonderful thing, but it requires some discipline. People addicted to compulsive behavior or blackmailed by society's pressures are not free. They are slaves to their lack of personal convictions.

Now that you have graduated, you can begin to make these decisions largely for yourself. As a Christian, however, you are voluntarily committed to the truth of Scripture that you are not your own, but you are bought with a price. To be a Christian implies that you believe that because God made you, he knows how to fix you and to guide you into paths of greatest happiness and fulfillment. His commandments were not given to make you miserable but to insure the fullest expression of your humanity.

The Christian's college experience can be a party, but it must be the kind Jesus would attend. However, he was never a wet blanket, even when Peter and the guys went "skinny dipping." Never think of Jesus as a person walking around in flip-flops and a bathrobe with sheep following him, but try to see him as a friend who loves you more than any other and as such smiles at your occasional failures, desires your well-being, and more fully understands your humanity than anyone you've ever known. With Jesus you can kick back, take off the shoes of your mind, and really relax. Remember, one of the fruits of the Spirit is joy.

Discipline and Freedom: Practical Tips

Back in the olden days—what you might call the 1960s—a song popular with many young people was titled, "Freedom Isn't Free." Among other things it spoke of the price in human lives paid by young Americans in securing our freedom. When I'm in Washington, D.C., I often go to Arlington National Cemetery and look at all of the grave markers to remind myself of this truth.

There are other costs that each of us must pay for our own freedom. I learned one of these lessons in my first year of college. I can't even begin to describe to you how exciting I found college to be. I had a dorm room, two roommates, my own hours, exciting and sometimes strange guys down the hall, and all kinds of

> *"The thought of being told to do something or of being regimented was a put-off to me in high school because it was a kind of 'need thing.' When I first arrived at college, I decided to turn over a new leaf. I got new notebooks, put my schedule on the wall, and decided I was really going to be in charge. That lasted about half a week until my old self took over. What I didn't realize was how many distractions there were—mostly procrastination. There's always something more fun to do than getting to work and studying. I'll bet almost everyone faces this during the first weeks, and some never recover. I'm doing better now, partly because I don't want to fall behind again like last semester."*

activities to attend. There were parties, informal get togethers in the student union, ball games, concerts, and most of all girls and dates. I was afraid to go to bed for fear I'd miss something! I literally was the last person in bed because of all of the action. Before long I found that I couldn't concentrate in classes. I'd go to sleep as soon as I tried to read, and I almost always had a headache. Suddenly it dawned on me that human beings need sleep.

Among many freshmen it is a kind of badge of honor to "pull all-nighters," that is, to stay up all night to "study." I found an all-night restaurant and bar that served sandwiches at three or four in the morning and felt like a character out of some detective story as I watched the night people and studied in the corner. Just before it killed me, I came to the conclusion that I had better do two things, and they have stuck with me for my entire life. I decided that I should be in bed before midnight if I was going to function the next day, and I bought an alarm clock and decided never to sleep beyond seven o'clock. I know this sounds like some kind of a sentence and very regimented, but the trade-off is worth it all. To have a clear mind and rested body is a most freeing experience.

You may not believe me, and most will try the old way first, but when you feel just about ready to roll over and go "toes up," and after you have passed out midsentence, try to remember the discipline of rest. Try to avoid the nap cycle. Most college students are not disciplined enough to go to bed, and so they often nap several times a day. This mixes up your nights and days and makes study difficult, because you are often groggy. You also often sleep through meals and then have to spend extra money going to restaurants or the ever-present candy and snack machines. This is not good nutrition and accounts for what (especially in girls) many call the "freshman sixteen"—those pounds that often appear the first semester (not to mention the extra Clearasil). If you push through the afternoon blahs or go for a walk or jog, you will begin to control your body rather than be its slave. Mark Twain once said, "In hell it's always 3:00 in the afternoon." He probably learned that in his freshman year of college.

Closely related to the discipline of the body is the wise use of time. As many have pointed out, everyone has twenty-four hours a day. However, we very soon discover that some are able to accomplish a great deal more than others. How do they do it? Well, it usually is not that they have more ability, nor is it magic. It is usually a matter of discipline and not wasting time. The overwhelmingly greatest disease of college students is procrastination—putting off unpleasant tasks and avoiding deadlines until it's either too late or the pressure is so great that they almost go under.

Several things will help you overcome this when you arrive at college. First, you will need a calendar and a daily schedule. If you have a calendar with each month marked off in squares by the weeks and days, you can take a red marker and show all of your test days and due dates for papers and projects in each class. You can count back from each of these and begin reading, projects, and test preparation ahead of time. It's a good idea to put your daily class schedule on your calendar so you can see what you have ahead of you at a glance. Another good idea is to have a weekly datebook that you are able to carry in your book bag or in your pocket. Don't get a very little one, because your social commitments, class assignments, and other reminders will fill it too quickly.

Right now, this probably seems a little too much like being organized, but it will free your mind to think rather than use it for a storehouse. You will also be free from forgetting. I have a rule that if it isn't written down, it isn't a commitment. It is embarrassing and also damaging to your reputation to miss appointments and forget commitments.

I would also suggest that you keep a "To Do" list for each day. When you complete something you simply cross it off the list. Eventually you will have a great sense of accomplishment as you get things done and out of the way.

When I was a college freshman I got a summer job delivering supplies to restaurants. My immediate superior and the driver of the truck (I was the flunky who lifted the other end of things) was a senior at Notre Dame University, married, and a terrific guy. He impressed me by his high moral standards and loyalty to his wife. However, I learned the best thing from watching him eat pie at lunch. He would always eat the crust first and work his way toward the point. After several lunches I decided to challenge him because this simply didn't seem natural to me. Doesn't everyone eat pie point first? His answer changed my life. He said, "Think about it. If you eat the point first, the last taste you have in your mouth is dry crust. I save the point till last so I have the best taste in my mouth all afternoon." That made sense, and for me has formed a life principle. Get the unpleasant things out of the way first so you can enjoy your free time. If you put the undesirable things off, not only do they not get done, but the dread of them ruins the time you do have.

Sometime into the third or fourth month it usually dawns on most students that an unusual odor is coming from their room. This is usually a combination of apple cores under the dresser, mold growing on uneaten pizza, and dirty socks. In a zoo a keeper comes by every day and hoses down the cage, rinsing all of the peanut shells down the drain along with the other refuse. Residence halls do not provide this service. There is no "Rent–A–Mother" service to come by and empty the hamper or hang up your clothes. In high school many kids experience the magic of just taking off their clothes and dropping them on the floor. As if by miracle, they reappear laundered, neatly folded in drawers, or pressed and on hangers in the closet.

Upon arriving at college this miracle ceases, and many students look a lot like unmade beds until they learn to do these things for themselves. Keeping clothes properly hung on hangers and laundry stored away until it can be laundered, as well as figuring out how to use the laundry equipment, can greatly add to making your room a place conducive to human habitation and academic accomplishment. The animal-house idea of college life may be funny and provide some distraction for junior high kids at the local theater, but no one can succeed in a serious academic environment over a long period of time this way. Cleanliness may not really be next to godliness, but it surely will make you into a more successful student and more pleasant to be around.

Keeping things picked up, folded, and put away will greatly simplify your life. A regular time to do laundry and taking some reading along will make the time spent more efficient. Setting aside time for these tasks and getting them behind you makes life simpler and also reflects on your character. If you maximize your day by using the odd hours between classes for study, you will have more free time in the evenings. Most students finish a class and then go to the student union or some hangout and blow the time until their next class. They store up all of their work until the evening hours instead of using these daily opportunities. It's a great feeling to be caught up so that you can goof off in the evening rather than feel oppressed by unfinished work.

Good study habits will save you more time in college than any other thing, because studying is what it's all about. Few students can do much studying in their rooms because of distractions like music, bull sessions, water fights, pranks, and the temptation to get a few minutes of sleep, or as they say, "just a few z's."

A neat idea is to stake out your own territory someplace away from distractions. Libraries are good for this. If you find a favorite spot where you will not be tempted to watch everyone who walks by, especially the opposite sex, it will help. Though a window is nice, it is also a temptation toward daydreaming. It's kind of like a bird selecting a place for a nest, away from the wind, rain, and predators. You need a place away from noise, friends, music, and time wasters. A solid hour in this environment is worth five in the wrong place. You won't miss anything; in fact, you will free up quality time to do what you want to do. Remember, discipline is the best friend of freedom.

If you learn to take good notes in class in a neat manner, you won't have to waste your time recopying them or copying from other people's notes. When you read your textbooks, learn to pick out the key words and ideas and highlight them. You can review at much greater speed if you do this thoroughly and well.

Be realistic about your needs. You probably can't really sit and study three to four hours straight, especially as a freshman. Put in a solid hour, do something else for a while, and come back and hit it again. It doesn't help just to stare at your books. You have to understand what you're reading.

One of the smartest things I ever did was to learn to read faster. I took a speed-reading course and read several books and articles on the subject. Eventually I learned to focus on whole sentences rather than one word at a time and more than tripled my speed. When you are required to read a great deal, this can save a lot of your time. Learning to focus your attention on the task at hand and giving it your full attention will revolutionize your study time.

On this subject, my student friends really got into it. Here are some of their best shots.

> "It's much easier to take your grade point average (GPA) down than to bring it up. Don't sluff off and get behind. Stick with the good habits that got you where you are, and don't coast."

> "Don't study all the time. Have some fun. When you do study all of the time, it's kind of like an obsession, which really is about fear and being tense. You've got to relax so that you can give your best effort when you do study. People who study all the time really don't. They actually fret and excuse themselves from real life."

> "Study hard during the week so you can have a weekend."

"Decide you are going to do it, and do it. It's like running; you've got to 'guts it out' past the barrier, and then you enjoy it."

"Try to get away from people. Interruptions are always lurking around the dorm, so read, socialize, and sleep there, but study somewhere else."

"Keep up daily and prepare for class. If you fake it, it's more work than preparation."

"Avoid escaping through sleeping away your life. A lot of college students waste most of the day when they are not in class by sleeping and avoiding the unpleasant."

"Take good notes—not every word—but good enough that you can really review what was said and understand it."

"Communicate with your professors. Find out what they want and discuss it with them. Try to make a good impression. If they think you are smart, they will grade you better even when you don't do as well. They think you just had a bad day."

"Participate in class. It keeps you awake and focused and helps the professor to distinguish you from other people. They are human and appreciate people who are interested in what they are saying."

"Consider getting a tape recorder for guest lecturers."

"Read classics and good books. Read, read, read—it will help you to learn to think."

(See the select reading list in Appendix B of this book.)

9

Spiritual Discipline

G rowing into a mature faith is part of what happens during college for many young people. It is often in college where they learn the habits that will go with them through life. One thing that will be a great help is to get a good study Bible if you do not already have one. There are several on the market that you may find helpful. Go to a Christian bookstore; or, if you are at a Christian college, you will find several options at the college bookstore. Select one in a translation that you enjoy. You might want to get a New International Version for study and a Living Bible for diversity in your devotions, for example. It is helpful to have maps and a concordance so you can look up places and words.

> *"One thing I found out is that you can lose your spiritual edge even when you are taking Bible courses. Studying about the Bible and Bible study are two different things. I found out that my spiritual life takes effort, and I can't get it by osmosis. For me the most important thing is that I'm part of an accountability group where we check on each other. Sometimes it seems to take too much time, but that's when I most need help. The spiritual life is a battle for me, and if I slack off, I lose, and I know it."*

Going away to college is a great time to turn over a new leaf and make some new vows. I have an understanding with our students that they can ask me any day, "What did you get from the Word today?" This keeps me on track and it helps them remember, too. Make a new habit of Bible study as part of your daily schedule.

It's a good idea to find a time and a place where you meet the Lord each day. There are many good ways to have devotions. One that has worked for me is to begin with a prayer in which I ask God to speak to me from his Word. I then read until something speaks to me. I stop and reread the passage and attempt to apply the principle or command to my life. I then go over my life and relationships and ask the Lord to help me to make this teaching a part of my life and relationships. Lately I've been going over the same passage for several days and then moving on to the next verses when I feel I have really understood and applied what I have read.

Another method I have found helpful is to read a section that contains a complete thought or teaching. Sometimes it is one chapter, but other times it may run on into another. Sometimes it is one paragraph. I then ask several questions: To whom is this addressed? What was the situation that prompted it to be written? What was the larger context in which it takes place? Are there specific commands or warnings in the passage? Were these specific to the context or are they universal for all Christians? What changes in attitude, behavior, or mindset are suggested to me? I then ask God to make these real to me and help me to live up to the ideals or standards of the text, such as to ask forgiveness of God as well as of people if I have wronged them. I would suggest that you go through a book at a time beginning in the New Testament, preferably 1 John and 1 and 2 Timothy for starters, then on to the rest in a systematic way.

Another pattern that I have found helpful is to read a passage from the Old Testament, a chapter from Psalms or Proverbs, and a chapter from the New Testament each day, once again asking the Holy Spirit to make specific lessons jump out to me that I can take through the day.

A helpful pattern for prayer for me has been the ACTS approach. You may already use it. I find it keeps me focused and also keeps my prayers from being just a list of gimmicks such as "Give me this and please give me that."

Begin with A for adoration and spend a period of time simply worshiping God for who he is and praise him for his person, creation, character, power, and nature. This helps you focus on the real object of your prayer, God himself.

C is for confession. In this part of your prayer you confess your sins and seek Christ's forgiveness for your transgressions in word, deed, and attitude. Try to focus on the seriousness of sin by remembering the suffering of Christ and what he experienced for your redemption and forgiveness. I always pray this prayer of David: "Search me, O God, and know my heart . . . and see if there is any wicked way in me, and lead me in the way everlasting" (Ps. 139:23–24).

T is for thanksgiving. During this period of my devotions I try to concentrate on all of the things for which I am thankful. This is for most of us a very long list if we think about it, and a source of real blessing if we simply stop to acknowledge what God has done. I start with the gift of life itself and move through all of the many areas of provision that I'm prone to take for granted. For instance, I was raised in a loving, caring home. My parents really sacrificed for me when I was growing up. I was able to go to college. I had a pretty healthy body and a sound mind. Somehow I found my wife, Janie, from among all the women in the world. We have great kids, enjoy each other, and so on and on. I can be thankful for really thousands of things. It's amazing how it helps when you are tempted to feel sorry for yourself to do what the song says: "Count your blessings, name them one by one."

The S in ACTS stands for supplication. That's a long word and conveniently starts with S, but it simply means request. It is the process of bringing your concerns to Christ and asking for his partnership, guidance, help, or provision for yourself and other people!

Most of us have little problem with the business of asking. That's why I like this approach to prayer. Asking comes last, after I have put things into perspective through adoration, confession, and thanksgiving. As we pray we can also bring the concerns of others to God and by this very act move ourselves away from our self-centeredness to become more caring people. A wise person once said, "Someone all wrapped up in himself is a very small package." We've all known people like that and need to work on the tendency in ourselves. This is the time that we can even pray for our enemies and, as the Bible says, "those who despitefully use us." We are amazed when after we have prayed for people we don't like, we begin to understand them better and don't have to carry the heavy baggage of hate, grudges, getting even, and feeling sorry for ourselves.

Daily prayer is to the soul, personality, and mind what a good shower is to the body. We become refreshed, invigorated, and able to face life with greater strength and resolve. A person's interior life is in many ways more central to successful living than the exterior. You are doubtless aware of and perhaps part of the current "hard-body" emphasis of this generation. The goal of spiritual discipline is to be strong and robust in our souls so that we have the reserve we need to face life's challenges.

One additional tip I would offer in this regard that has been helpful to me, especially in the area of motivation and getting over moods and depression, is to read biography. I try to read one useful biography at least every three months. This last year I read another Lincoln biography as well as one each on Leo Tolstoy, William Jennings Bryan, and Borden of Yale. Reading about the lives of great people is a lift to our lives and inspires us to take on greater challenges.

People who have accomplished anything of value in life have had obstacles, disappointments, reversals, handicaps, and failures as well as successes. You can learn from their mistakes as well as their accomplishments. For me that is a source of spiritual strength and example. If they could do it, why not me? Or you? As coaches say to all athletes, "They put their pants on one leg at a time, just like us."

That's one reason I like to study Bible characters. Often I will take my Bible and read everything recorded about a particular individual such as David, Samson, Sarah, Paul, Peter, Mary, Timothy, Luke, or any other character. What is neat is that they were real people. God does not make them sound like Superheroes. He tells it like it is, and still he loved them and uses them as examples. This keeps me from letting my Christian life become spooky and full of unrealistic religious ideas. God made us, understands us, loves us, forgives us, instructs us, rescues us, disciplines us, but never forsakes us. He is a "friend who sticks closer than a brother," so it's a good idea to really become acquainted with him by learning from the Bible what he is like.

God does not expect things of you that you cannot do. True discipleship is giving all that you know of yourself to all that you know of God. You cannot do more. As life goes on you will understand more of yourself and you will also gain new insight into the nature and character of God. Christian maturity is a matter of sincere commitment of yourself as you now are to your best understanding of God's will. You will have great opportunity for spiritual growth during these next ten years of your life. Don't miss it.

My student friends made some suggestions that made a lot of sense to me, especially since they are right in the middle of what's going on.

"Set aside a time and a place for devotions, or you will fail."

"Make a covenant with another person or persons to keep each other accountable by asking each other how it is going. If you have a covenant, you won't resent each other asking."

"Keep a diary or journal of your spiritual journey and review it each month to see if you are growing."

"Don't just skip around in the Bible. You won't get anything out of that approach."

"Don't try to pray and read when you are dog-tired. You will read things over and over and they won't sink in."

"It's better to be regular than to take a long time. One thing that you can apply each day is all anyone can handle."

"Keep a prayer list and record when prayers are answered. It will really amaze you at what God does."

Relationships, Friendships, and Marriage

et's face it, there is a lot of discussion in today's world about singleness and human sexuality and questions as to whether a person should be married at all. Many of the voices say in essence, "Since you can get sex whenever you want it, and because career opportunities often demand mobility, why get married and tie yourself down to commitments that often end in divorce or the stifling of individual plans?" These things are discussed on every level, from The Oprah Winfrey Show to college forums, and provide no end to opinions on diverse options. When all is said and done, however, most people end up in a marriage, start a family, and more or less work things out in the traditional framework. Contrary to

"It's really hard to overstate the feelings we had about the boy-girl thing when we went away to college. Somehow it seemed that everything about our personal identity was tied up in our attractiveness to the opposite sex. It's not so much that I felt ready to choose a life partner or that I really had a need for sexual experience. It's just that there was this curiosity: Could I really attract the neat guys, and would they see me as someone to spend their life with? If I were really honest, I'd have to say I'd like for guy after guy to fall head over heels in love with me and propose, so that I could say, 'I'm sorry. I'm not ready to settle down yet. Maybe later.' It's not that I would like to hurt them, but I'd like to know I'm desirable. Somehow I'd like to meet a lot of guys, have a lot of fun, and then make my choice at the last minute so that I'd not miss 'Mr. Right.' I've prayed about it, but secretly I'm a little bit afraid that God's choice may be a little too responsible or stuffy. You know what I mean. I'm not wanting to live outside the will of God, but I don't want to be ordinary and trapped. I had all these thoughts as I went away to college. Now I think I was pretty immature then. I feel a lot more secure now, and deep down I believe it will work out."

the more flamboyant opinions explored in the media, most married people are happy and fulfilled. Now that you are graduated you are in the chapter of your life when dating, engagement, and marriage are usually pursued and decisions are made.

It is almost impossible in today's complex, diverse culture to discuss these issues without some value-based framework in which to make decisions and pursue goals. For the Christian young person the choices are still varied and complex; however, there are guidelines and prohibitions given to us by God that help us to proceed with confidence, anticipation, and hope. It's great to know that God made us and therefore knows what is best for us. In recent years many surveys and studies have been done on the subject of personal happiness, fulfillment, and satisfaction with life, marriage, and family. To the amazement of those who advocate alternate lifestyles, people in monogamous Christian marriage come out as most satisfied, happy, and fulfilled. This should be no surprise to us, since God is a loving heavenly Father who wants the best for his children. So let's not move too fast toward marriage, but let's talk a lot about the process of dating, friendship, and ultimately the subject of selecting a life partner and mate.

The word *mate* implies male and female. This is true when buying bolts and nuts, electrical plugs and receptacles, watching songbirds, or building a life together. Male and female are made for each other and they fit within the created order.

You live in an age when both men and women are bombarded by the arguments of the homosexual community and other people who often argue with great concern for the fair and civil treatment of diversity in our lives. As Christians we must be committed to kindness, civility, and fairness toward this vocal minority, and we must deplore any violation of their rights under the law or as persons loved by God. We are not obligated, however, nor are we allowed by Scripture, to accept homosexual behavior as normative or as an alternate lifestyle for Christian persons.

If you should find yourself confused about your own sexual identity, I would strongly urge you to discuss this issue with your pastor or another person you believe is prepared to help you sort it out from a Christian and caring perspective. It is not within the scope of this short book to discuss this at any depth except to say that almost all persons, male and female, have questions on the subject of homosexuality and, depending on their life experience or the voices of those around them, have times of worry or concern about their orientation. This is a normal part of growing up and in no way suggests gender confusion or homosexual orientation. A rather large and growing literature on the subject is available in Christian bookstores to help guide you if this is a troubling issue.

For the overwhelming majority of college-age men and women there is a strong urge to explore the mystery and excitement of male-female relationships and human sexuality. For the Christian there is a sanctity to sexuality. It was God's idea, and he speaks a great deal about it in the Bible.

While at college you will be pretty much self-regulated. Even if your college has guidelines such as separate residence halls or floors for men and women and you are not faced with the challenge of coed dorms, you can still circumvent the intention of your parents and school administrators and lead an immoral life. As I discuss this issue with students, they tell me that the main problems are in four areas:

1. They have never experienced such freedom before, with no one there to make sure they get in at a proper time or to monitor their dating behavior.
2. They have never been in an atmosphere where there were so many attractive people of the opposite sex who also have this freedom.
3. There is a fear that if they don't grab a partner right away, all of the potential partners will be claimed by someone else.
4. They are frightened and insecure, being away from home for the first time, and are tempted to get involved with someone else experiencing the same sense of

dislocation. Their mutual need for security draws them to each other.

For the Christian young person it is important to remember that the whole issue of the Christian faith hangs on the issue of ownership. When we commit ourselves to Christ, we are in essence saying that we want him to be the center of our lives and to take us over. Scripture says we are not our own, for we are bought with a price. The price, of course, is the price Christ paid by dying for us on the cross. He in essence purchased us from the damnation of our sins and made us his very own. We are told our bodies are temples of the Holy Spirit. What a Christian does with his or her own body is not just a personal matter but of concern to Christ. Many Christian students, aware of the physical temptations inherent in male-female relationships and aware of the social and psychological pressures and expectations put on young adults today, pray about these issues before their dates. Because they have made it a habit to pray about all things from school work to personal attitudes, they ask God before they go out on a date to help them to remember their Christian commitment and to have the strength to listen to his voice.

This is not being pious; it is simply smart. Other students tell me that they often pray in the car before they leave the campus together, for their safety while driving and that all the events of the evening will be in God's care. Since human sexuality is such a big issue in every movie, book, play, courtroom, and television magazine, it seems like a good idea to let God have a place in it. Just because you have freedom and no one is around to watch you does not mean you have to use your freedom wrongly. The joy of freedom is that by allowing God to participate in it, you are more fulfilled.

Being in an atmosphere where there are so many people with this same freedom available to them sometimes provides great social pressures. There is often an unspoken undercurrent of expectation that seems to shout, "Hey! Let's party!" In many settings this implies alcohol, sex, and drugs. Once again, you can leave Christ at the door or invite him to be a part of it all. Some young people make the mistake of thinking that all God wants to be a part of is a worship service with the music played slowly in a minor key. This is a distortion. The Bible says, "Whatever you do in word or deed, do all in the name of the Lord Jesus, giving thanks to God the Father through Him" (Col. 3:17). All things certainly include your social life.

One thing that Christian college students do today far better than in my student days is to hold one another accountable. Rather than be influenced by negative peer groups, they create their own positive peer groups. They discuss their lives and try to plan activities that are creative, exciting, unpredictable, and wholesome—the kind that do not produce regrets and do not produce a hangover.

Another thing that can reduce the panic about all of the available people being taken and you being left over is to put greater emphasis on group activities where everyone is not paired off. It makes a more relaxed and mature atmosphere if you can develop a shifting group of men and women made up of more or less the same people but open to new people and not obliging the old ones. These "compatibility groups" can provide the environment in which relationships are allowed to develop without the necessity of going steady or being put out of circulation by the attitude that "he (she) belongs to him (her) because they dated last week." This "they-own-them" atmosphere makes it difficult to get acquainted with others and makes many fearful of dating altogether because they don't want to be trapped.

Creating your own peer group and discussing these issues on occasion, not in a formal way but as part of the ongoing table talk and bull sessions, can be greatly helpful to lower the tension of feeling rushed and trapped and can provide a great place to cultivate lasting friendships (and in many cases a life partner) in a relaxed and comfortable manner. Another good tension relaxer is to commit the entire issue to God and believe that he will indeed provide the right person for you in his own good time. This is one of the most difficult things to do. Many young people have less trouble trusting God for their eternal salvation than they do trusting him to find a mate. The God who made the universe can doubtless handle this important assignment.

When you think about it, being in an environment with many young adults over a period of four years gives opportunity for many friendships and much better possibilities for choice than getting in a hurry and locking into the deal the first month. It could be the right choice, but the chances are less likely.

The possibility of being drawn together through mutual need is both the most natural and the most dangerous. It is very natural to be insecure, lonely, and frightened in new surroundings. College is new in just about every way. The place where you live, the food you eat, the places where you hang out, the classes you take, the expectations, the competition, and the people are all new. Not to be somewhat apprehensive would truly require special self-confidence, and few have that. When two people, each feeling disoriented and alone, see something of familiarity or common interest, they often huddle together for mutual support. There is nothing wrong with this. It only becomes undesirable when the two people freeze in this condition, kill off their other options, and build on their fears in the name of love.

When people do this, it is like setting something in concrete that will probably need changing when one or both have grown and become less afraid. Many relationships like this break up after time, and that's all right. It's unfortunate, however, when the relationship has resulted in a premature marriage and the pain and complexity of divorce scars the two persons for life. Far better to recognize and acknowledge insecurity and fear for what they are and even find a friend to help you through, than to mistake these feelings for the kind of compatibility that is required for lasting love such as is found in marriage.

College is a terrific time to play the field, to get to know many people, to avoid immature and complicating relationships—especially sexual promiscuity—and trust God to make things really click with the right person for you. Finding the right mate with shared goals and values, whose faith commitment is complementary and enriching to your own, is more possible in the college context than in any context I know.

Like so much of life, this issue ties directly back to your faith. If you are God's creation and he has revealed himself as caring for and loving you, then you can be confident that if you apply the principles taught in Scripture about chastity, patience, and trust, God will help you in the selecting of a life partner or in making you fulfilled and happy as a single person. Settling the faith issue and turning the title to your life over to him takes the panic out of the dating game, but it does require a trust in God that is the result of spiritual growth and is not automatic. Many young people panic and take the plunge before they have reached the level of maturity that they really need. The important ingredients are patience, faith in yourself and God, and a willingness to read the warning signals in your courtship that will only amplify after the wedding. "As now, so then" is a wise proverb in this choice.

There was no hesitation on the part of students to offer advice on the issue of dating and romance.

"Relationships will be lifelong, so be careful that you don't build regrets into them. I like to think that one can have really deep friendships with the opposite sex without sexual overtones."

"Beware of the idea that you are here to find a life partner; maybe so, maybe not. But it is not like an Easter-egg hunt where you can look and look and come home with an empty basket. If the right person is around, I think, you will find him or her. Otherwise, wait."

"College dating can be oppressive. You spend all day together, eating, studying, ball games. Eventually sex follows because you are bored, not because it's right. Then it becomes boring! It's a good idea to limit time together, even though it's easy to be like you're glued together."

"Pace yourself. My boyfriend took me away from everyone, and when we broke up I was disconnected and lonely."

"If you get too involved too soon and break up, you feel angry and crushed. Save total commitment for marriage, not dating."

"I found out that the reason I was so possessive was not love but my insecurity and fear that I was not good enough for her. I was jealous, not so much of the other guys as I was afraid of being alone. I decided to get my own act together before I allowed myself to date one person exclusively."

"I want to be mature enough to give my true self and not fear rejection and play a role."

"I think there are seasons in life. Right now I am happy to have relationships around events, ball games, projects, and then get more serious later."

"When it comes right down to it, you have to trust God in this issue. Think of all the possibilities of making a mistake. I don't know how, but I think God will guide me in this if I trust him."

11

What Do You Want to Be?

What do you want to be when you grow up?" is the question most often asked of children by adults. To be sure, it is often merely a way of saying something to fill the silence between the generations. What they mean is, "I'm interested in you and don't know what to say to a small person." Now the adult-kid game is over and you have to come up with a real answer. Being Batman or the Cookie Monster probably won't cut it.

The sense of urgency and finality of the choice need not be quite as frightening as it seems to many. Actually, most people start in a particular career and change several times throughout their lifetimes. I once read that more than half of all the people

95

"I really felt pushed when I began college. They want you to declare a major, and the truth is, I wasn't ready. I knew I would eventually have to earn a living, but I wasn't ready to take the first step. It felt sort of like making the first move in chess. All the others start to fall in line, and you can kind of see the end before all the moves are made. I felt like that about my classes, and even though my folks weren't really all that pushy, their questions seemed to say that it was about time for me to begin to give serious thought to what I'd like to do with the rest of my life. What I really wanted was to be left alone for a while and sort of survey the territory, but it seemed as though everybody was saying, 'It's your move. Plan the rest of your life.'"

listed in *Who's Who in America* are on the list for something they decided to do after they were forty-five years old. So there's hope and not quite so much need to panic.

Most young people have some general idea of what they would like to do by observing others or admiring a particular person. This is great, except that none have been exposed to all of the possibilities because of age and limited experience. Because few people want to make career choices before they are satisfied that they have exhausted all of the options, most young people want to postpone making a final decision. I always find it interesting when I talk to college freshmen that the most common major is "undeclared. With the exception of students who are very focused, such as pre-med or engineering majors, most feel comfortable selecting something rather broad and then narrowing it down as they are exposed to more possibilities through reading, talking to other students, or interaction with professors about their inclinations and aptitudes. Even pre-med and engineering majors discover that there are literally dozens of specific options within their broader fields. Two of our best basketball players have chosen to teach in elementary school because they came to the conclusion that young kids need strong male models who have the courage of their Christian convictions. Neither really thought of this option before they were exposed to the great opportunities in their fields in college.

Most colleges have a number of general-studies courses that are required of all students for graduation. Usually you can take these courses in the first two years and thus postpone making a final choice of your major. This allows you time to learn more about yourself and also to become exposed to various options and interests that perhaps you were not aware of before you arrived at college. May articles are being written today in which employers suggest that what they really want when they hire young people into the work force are people with a broad education who possess solid reasoning skills, who can write and communicate clearly, and who have interpersonal skills that enable them to relate well to others.

Also, most employers want people to be computer literate and able to use today's high-tech communication tools. Students with proficiency in a second language are specifically sought in certain industries and businesses that work in the international marketplace. Usually companies have their own training programs for specific tasks within the company. Increasingly, young people are pursuing graduate degrees to qualify for certain fields and more demanding occupations. As you mature and become more aware of your aptitudes, opportunities, and the specific requirements of various occupations, these things will become familiar to you. It is probably a good idea to take one step at a time and make each decision on the basis of knowledge you gain with each step.

Sometimes if you try to think about all of these steps at one time, they are unnecessarily threatening and simply put too much pressure on you too soon. It is a good thing to realize that all of these seemingly complicated things are done by ordinary human beings like you and that you've always managed to compete with others along the way. These new people and challenges at each stage of life are no different from the people and challenges that you have faced so far in your personal growth.

My greatest fears always took place in gym class. There we would be, all lined up in our gym shorts, shivering a little, while the gym teacher said, "Okay, you guys! We're going to run today. I want you to do four laps, and the last guys to finish are in for a little surprise." I'd look over all of the guys and pretty well know which ones would finish first, because I had known them all since kindergarten. I remember saying to myself a thousand times in these situations. "If they can do it, so can I. I may not finish first, but I won't finish last, and even if I do, somehow I'll make it." Frankly, all of life has turned out much like that for me. If someone else can do it, so can I. I'm not going to be intimidated and lose by default.

I see many young people who would rather not try than not excel. This is a formula for rationalization and failure, and though it may protect their egos in the short term, it will eventually rob them of any long-term happiness and success. Everyone has apprehensions. You are not alone, nor are you weird for being afraid. Everyone had to start someplace, and you are no different. In fact, you are probably above average if you have taken the time to read this book.

In most colleges there are career centers and faculty advisors available to assist you in evaluating your ideas and options.

They will be willing to provide information about various fields as well as what is required to meet their standards. It is also useful to take advantage of college testing centers that are able to help you evaluate what subjects and areas of interest best fit your capabilities. The great thing about life is that there are opportunities suited to each of our tastes and preferences, and if we take the time and effort to explore the options, they will usually surface.

For Christian young people there is the additional benefit of being able to let God in on the choice and to pray for guidance and open doors from him. As one student told me, "it's amazing how much closer the coincidences get to each other when you pray about things." He was speaking of the sense of God's hand on his shoulder and the fact that things seemed to work out so much better when he prayed and asked for God's intervention. It is certainly not a bad idea to attempt to be sensitive to the subtle nudging of the Holy Spirit and to watch for his red lights and green lights as you make choices and decide important things about your future.

It has always been my belief that we are God's creation and he loves us supremely, to the point of sending his Son to die for us, and that it follows that he wants us to be happy and fulfilled in our lives. If we attempt to be obedient to him and make our choices with his will in mind, then our place of greatest happiness will be closest to his will. If you are truly committed to Christ as you live each day, and if you truly desire to be the person God intended you to be, it is reasonable to expect that he will guide you into the place of greatest fulfillment and joy. If you ignore God and seek only selfish or convenient ends, then you may launch out into uncharted waters and end up in shipwreck far away from God's best for you.

I have never met a person who felt betrayed or disappointed in the long run for having followed his or her sense of God's direction. Don't be afraid to aim high and ask God for the best. The greatest danger is not in aiming too high and missing the mark. The greatest danger is in having no goals and not asking God for the strength and help to achieve your dreams.

Costs: How Can I Afford College?

About the time you entered high school, your folks probably began to break out in cold sweats every time they thought about college expenses for you. You, of course, were too busy adjusting to high school and its demands to think too much about it. Some students have heard their parents talk so much about how expensive college is that they have given up on the idea altogether because they feel college is beyond their financial reach.

Each college has its own department devoted to assisting students with paying for their college education, usually known as the office of financial aid. It deals with scholarships, student loans, government grants, institutional grants, and work-study opportunities.

"I really didn't know much about my parents' financial situation other than the fact that we seemed to get along pretty well. But when we started talking about college, my folks told me that my school bill would be about one-fourth of what my dad makes each year, and it really scared me. I think they were scared, too, and so when we got our financial-aid report back from the school, we were really quite surprised. I'm going to have some loans to repay, but I believe in the long run it will be worth it. Anyway, it's the only way we can afford it, and it's for my benefit. I've learned a lot about money since coming to college, and I think it's been good for me."

The process for getting financial aid for the prospective college freshman starts at the beginning of the senior year of high school. If your school's counseling office does not automatically send them to all seniors, stop in and pick up a copy of the Free Application for Federal Student Aid (FAFSA). (Prior to 1993 a fee was charged for filing the application.) The deadline for submitting this is usually in mid-February.

This is your initial application and is basic for all financial aid. It is a standard form which contains a series of detailed questions on your family's financial situation similiar to and in conjunction with those on their income tax return. This information is computed according to a federal-government formula that determines the amount your family can afford to pay toward college expenses. It is shown on your Student Aid Report (SAR), and you will receive a copy. You can then request your SAR to be sent to each college—public or private—to which you apply for admission.

Sometimes parents resent this form, for it reminds them of applying for a bank loan or mortgage. But it is wise for them to fill it out carefully, because if they don't they may overlook some important considerations.

When my children went to college, I filled out the financial aid form for my daughter and found out that not much aid was available to our family. I did not realize when our second child enrolled in college that a credit was given for having two children in college at the same time. We were eligible for some aid, but because I was somewhat angry and careless, we missed this opportunity. So much for Dad's bad attitude!

Next the college's financial aid office takes over. When it receives a copy of your SAR, it determines your unmet need, or difference between what your SAR says you can afford to pay and what your actual expenses will be at that college. It, too, will ask specific financial questions when you apply for admission and will take into consideration your family's circumstances. Then it will go to work to try to help you fill your unmet need with federal, state, and private grants, with scholarships, loans, work-study programs, and other resources at its disposal. This is the financial package it will offer you. The process need not be fearsome to you, for colleges treat students with financial need very well. Each year that you return to college you will have had to file an FAFSA the previous March.

If you are among the lower income families, government grants are available according to your need. Grants are good, because you don't have to pay them back. They are like scholarships, which work the same way. Scholarships are offered by most colleges to reward you for good work in high school and to help the college maintain the proper mix of students that they are looking for. Most want a balance of very good students with those who will have to develop study skills and catch up while in college. Some of the best students are late bloomers and get serious after they graduate from high school. Many are very bright but have been careless or were able to do fine in high school without much work because there were so many mediocre students in their schools. Just because you have been a careless high school student does not mean that you cannot turn over a new leaf in college. Many do, and so can you if you decide to do it. Often Christian young people see this as a spiritual challenge and make a turnaround a matter of serious commitment and prayer.

Scholarships are given for many reasons by each college. Usually a page or two in the college catalog lists the various categories. There are usually president's scholarships for the highest academic achievers and other categories below these such as trustee's scholarships, dean's scholarships, etc. Often families and benefactors of the college provide scholarships to students in specific categories. I got a scholarship available to an "Indiana male student studying for the ministry who could not go to college without this help." There are many of this type at most institutions, and the financial-aid counselors will make you aware of them.

In addition to grants and scholarships there are various student-loan programs backed by either the government or the institution. These are usually low-interest loans with generous payback schedules that make up the difference between what your family can afford right now and the available financial aid in grants and scholarships. In the school where I work, 70 percent of the students are on some form of financial aid. At many institutions the percentage is even higher. Don't feel embarrassed that you need financial aid. Almost everyone does in one form or another.

Each person has to estimate how much debt he or she can repay after graduation. If you look at the added value of a college education in terms of earning power, getting aid is still a very prudent path to take. I often tell students, "Just resist the temptation to visit a new-car dealer the first ten years after graduation and drive your 'beater' just a little longer. If you put away a typical car payment each month, you will have your college debt paid off with little pain. You simply have to postpone the gratification of driving a shiny little sports car a little longer."

Though it may in certain specific instances be utterly impossible for some to go to college, I will go so far as to say that if you truly want to do it, if you are willing to take the suggestions of the college counselors and advisors available to help you, and if you are willing to work and even take a little longer than some to achieve a degree, you can go to college in America.

Almost all families find that college expenses put extra strain on the family budget. For this reason most students try to help by earning all they can during the summer months to offset these costs. Each family is different, and each views the amount to be earned and what it goes for in different ways. Some parents are able to pay all of the fixed expenses such as tuition, fees, and room and board, and ask students to pick up the responsibility for their own spending money, books, entertainment, etc. Other students are unable to attend college unless they pay most of the expenses themselves.

Almost all colleges have what are called work-study programs. These are jobs on the campus that help the college to function more economically by employing students rather than professional staff. Many of these jobs are in the very departments in which students' majors are offered, and this provides not only employment for the students but valuable interaction with faculty and opportunities to become more acquainted with their fields of interest by reading for professors, grading papers, filing, setting up laboratories, and performing various other duties.

In addition, there are jobs in food service, housekeeping, and maintenance. These jobs are usually offered to the students with most need first and then become available to others as they are filled from a priority list. Students who really want to work will find that jobs are available if they are not too particular and are persistent to follow leads.

Besides subsidized work-study jobs are nearby off-campus jobs. These often pay more but can be more demanding of time and energy. Some, however, like night watchman or desk clerk are very good because students can study while they work. I had a job in a variety story that sold candy, newspapers, etc., and all I had to do was sit and wait for customers. I could often finish all of my reading assignments during my work hours and get paid for it. Not bad!

Probably the biggest reason why many students don't work is that they feel their schoolwork will be too demanding and they will not be able to do both at once. My observation is that most working students manage their time better than nonworking students and often get better grades than their nonworking friends. They simply waste less time. Another reason that some students don't want to have a job is that they are afraid it will rob them of their social life. There is no question that this can happen; however, I've noticed that working students usually develop relationships with fellow students in the workplace and enjoy friendships that are often closer and deeper than those developed on dates or goofing around with their friends. A job doesn't mean that your life at college is all work and no play. Most students find time for some of each.

Probably the most subtle resistance to work on many campuses is the unspoken bias that work is in some way demeaning, especially work like washing dishes or waiting on tables. For Christian young people this is not so much of a struggle, because they know that even Jesus was a servant to all. The temptation to snobbery or elitism is great among many privileged people around the world. One of the great things about America is that labor has dignity in our culture, and as a result we have the highest standard of living on the globe. If you have to work, be assured that many of the most outstanding people you know also worked at a part-time job in college, and most will say that not only was it okay but an excellent discipline and preparation for later life.

All of the students who made suggestions for this book work at some job while in school and on vacations. Here are some tips they felt would be helpful.

> "When I look over my checkbook at the end of the month when the bank sends back my canceled checks, I'm amazed that it is 'TOPPIT, TOPPIT, TOPPIT!' [TOPPIT is the name of a local pizza parlor—The Only Pizza Place In Town.] I realize that I really do blow a lot of unnecessary bucks on food. You can learn a lot from your canceled checks."

> "I'm a poor manager of money. If I have it, I'll spend it, so I have to stick to a strict budget."

> "There is a lot of stuff you don't *really* need."

> "Don't be afraid to say no if you can't afford it, like campus concerts and CDs. Your student activities fee pays for a lot of things if you just go, and besides, there are a lot of free things that are very good."

> "Don't be afraid to wait tables or to work in the dish room. Nobody looks down on you, and you can also get free food!"

"I dropped out for a year and worked. I'd recommend it to anyone. It was the best thing I ever did, because now I appreciate school a lot more."

"Learn to delay gratification. Do you need it? Really? Learn to get by."

"I just wasted a lot of time, anyway. I might as well work. It's a break in the routine and a kind of recreation, and I have friends I work with."

13

The Late Bloomer

Not everyone sails through high school at the same speed, nor do all realize their full potential as early as others. Many factors contribute to this, everything from family problems to personal motivation to personal likes and dislikes. The truth of the matter is that when people graduate from high school, the instruments that tell others who they are—grade point average, class rank, test scores, and extracurricular success—measure what they have attained to that point and not their real capacity. Because adolescence is often such a difficult time for many people, factors that have nothing to do with academic achievement often reflect themselves in classroom performance. Many young people have had struggles

"I was terrified when I applied for college. I made such a mess of things in my freshman and sophomore years of high school. I was just a goof-off and refused to get with the program. My folks warned me, and every teacher I had reminded me that my brother was a good student and wanted to know what my problem was. This made me all the more stubborn. When I looked at my class rank and GPA, I was embarrassed. The college-entrance people were pretty specific as to why I was accepted. It was because of my brother's reputation and my family. I was embarrassed to tell my friends that I was admitted on probation and couldn't have a car on campus that first year. Looking back now, I'm glad they got on my case, even though I nearly told them to hang it on the wall and nearly took off for California. It seems stupid now, but I guess I got off to the wrong start in high school."

with peer pressure, have become involved with the wrong friends, are sometimes handicapped by drug and alcohol problems, or, in the word of some kids today, simply have an "attitude." These things, though often outgrown and left behind in adulthood, can drastically affect the external measurements used to evaluate college entrance.

If for whatever reason you find yourself to have fallen behind and simply feel that there is no way to catch up, it is important for you to understand that there are many people around you who really care that you get a second chance and a fresh start. Usually your parents are eager to assist; and even if that is not so, college counselors are willing and desirous to help. Many schools are willing to help you by providing some form of remedial program or a probationary period for you to prove your resolve to change things. More selective schools will often take students as transfer students after they complete one or two successful years at an open-enrollment community college or junior college.

When you are turned down at a school of your choice, it is usually not a matter of its not wanting you. More likely it desires that you not be defeated by jumping into a competitive environment without the proper background. If admissions people suggest that you beef up your preparation with additional high school work or at a community college, they are making this suggestion for your own benefit. I've seen many students follow this advice and then succeed very well after they get used to college work and the expectations of professors. It is a good feeling and a real sense of accomplishment to prove to others who you really are and what you are made of. Those who simply give up and spend the rest of their lives making excuses or feeling that they got the muddy end of the stick often sentence themselves to unnecessary failure and unhappiness.

One of the first steps you need to take if you have fallen behind or believe you are capable of doing better than others think you can, is to admit how you feel and seek the help of people in the college admissions office. It's a good idea to gather up all of your courage and sit down with a counselor and lay all your cards on the table. Explain where you are and how you got there. Try not to make excuses and try your best to avoid a bad attitude. Try to believe that even though the advice you receive seems difficult, the counselor is doing his or her best to help you. If you run into an indifferent, matter-of-fact person who doesn't seem to care, try someone else. Say something like, "I talked with Mr. Smith and he didn't seem to see my options. Perhaps you can help me." Usually the next person will see your determination and sincere desire and make an effort in your behalf. Success, after all, isn't merely getting up but getting up every time you fall.

Many people would rather fail than try; then they find out they truly can't do the work. This is difficult to face, but in almost all cases, if one door closes, another will open up to the person who is willing to try.

Don't believe that you are a loser. God made you, and as a country song says, "God don't make no junk." There is a specific reason for all of us to be on the earth, and if you miss what God planned for you, all of the rest of us will be shortchanged, too. There is something special for you even if perhaps college is not your thing. The reason that I am encouraging the college option in this book is because for most people, it is the easiest and best way to realize their potential. Many have succeeded through the school of "hard knocks" and have contributed very greatly to our world, but they are the exception to the rule.

Each year at Taylor University we have a dinner in which we say thank you to a businessman who has given money to make it possible for students to attend college. Each year as he responds to our attempt to honor him, he mentions how he was unable to attend college but had to work in a factory as a young person. He worked very hard, and as a result of hard work and his personal genius he became quite well off. He impresses the students about the value of hard work and the fact that living in America has made it possible for him to be successful, but he encourages them to take advantage of the opportunities afforded today.

You can succeed. It may take a little longer if you start in the back of the pack, but you can be more than you now think you can be if you resolve to do so and if you allow God and those who love you to help.

It is very motivating to realize that you are a child of God and that he is on your side. Even when you feel alone, he's always with you, and even if no other person fully understands the reasons why you have struggled, God does.

Very few people I've ever known struggled like one of our students. He was born with a birth defect that caused him to miss months of school and fall behind. He had a speech difficulty and a spastic condition. He had social adjustment problems because of his limitations and sometimes was left out of things because the other kids were somewhat afraid of him. He began college and several times had to withdraw from classes because he was unable to keep up. Finally, after eight years of persistence, he received his diploma.

You may have seen something like this on TV or at school. When Gary got his diploma, everyone in his class stood to their feet and applauded. If ever a guy had a reason to quit and simply whine about the cards life dealt him, Gary had the right. Yet he refused to lose his goals even though he'd had a tough start. You can do it, too.

You've already crossed a great hurdle. You have graduated from high school. Congratulations! I hope as you move now into this next chapter of your life that the things in this book will be helpful. One thing I'm sure of: God is on your side and his help is available if you ask.

Appendix A

Christian College Consortium

Asbury College
201 North Lexington Avenue
Wilmore KY 40390-1198
606/858-3511

Bethel College
3900 Bethel Drive
St Paul MN 55112
612/638-6400

George Fox College
414 North Meridian
Newberg OR 97132
503/538-8383

Gordon College
Wenham MA 01984
617/927-2300

Greenville College
315 E College Avenue
Greenville IL 62246-0159
618/664-1840

Houghton College
One Willard Avenue
Houghton NY 14744
716/567-2211

Malone College
515 25th Street NW
Canton OH 44709
216/489-0800

Messiah College
Grantham PA 17027
717/766-2511

Seattle Pacific University
3307 Third Avenue West
Seattle WA 98119
206/281-2966

Taylor University
500 W Reade Avenue
Upland IN 46989-1001
317/998-2751

Trinity College
2077 Half Day Road
Deerfield IL 60015
312/948-8980

Wheaton College
Wheaton IL 60187
312/260-5000

Westmont College
955 LaPaz Road
Santa Barbara CA 93108
805/565-6000

Appendix B

Select Reading List for College Students: The Christian Faith and the Liberal Arts

This list of recommended books is prepared and periodically updated by a group of Taylor University faculty members and students. It identifies books which directly or indirectly seek to integrate Christian understanding and insight with one or more of the broad or liberal areas of learning. In general these books reflect the interest—and in some cases they also reflect the work—of the Taylor community.

Christian Apologetics
1. C. S. Lewis, *Mere Christianity*
2. Elton Trueblood, *A Place to Stand*
3. Elton Trueblood, *Philosophy of Religion*
4. G. K. Chesterton, *Orthodoxy*
5. G. K. Chesterton, *The Everlasting Man*
6. Paul Little, *Know Why You Believe*
7. John R. Stott, *Basic Christianity*
8. F. F. Bruce, *The Hard Sayings of Jesus*

Christian Biography
1. Ruth Tucker, *From Jerusalem to Irian Jaya: A Biographical History of Christian Missions*
2. Ruth Tucker and Walter Liefeld, *Daughters of the Church: Women and Ministry from New Testament Times to the Present*

3. Elisabeth Elliot, *Shadow of the Almighty: The Life and Testament of Jim Elliot*
4. Lindley Baldwin, *Samuel Morris*
5. Garth Lean, *Strangely Warmed: A Biography of John Wesley*
6. St. Augustine, *Confessions*
7. Richard Collier, *The General Next to God: The Story of William Booth and the Salvation Army*
8. John Pollack, *Hudson Taylor and Maria: Pioneers in China*
9. Catherine Marshall, *A Man Called Peter*
10. Mother Teresa, *My Life for the Poor*

Christian Classics
1. John Bunyan, *Pilgrim's Progress*
2. Dante, *The Divine Comedy*
3. John Milton, *Paradise Lost*
4. Edmund Spenser, *The Faerie Queen*
5. Alfred Tennyson, *Idylls of the King*

Christian Discipleship
1. Oswald Chambers, *My Utmost for His Highest*
2. Richard J. Foster, *Celebration of Discipline: The Path to Spiritual Growth*
3. Charles Sheldon, *In His Steps*
4. Dietrich Bonhoeffer, *The Cost of Discipleship*
5. Watchman Nee, *The Normal Christian Life*
6. William Law, *A Serious Call to a Devout and Holy Life*

Christian Meditation
1. Thomas á Kempis, *Imitation of Christ*
2. C. S. Lewis, ed., *George MacDonald, an Anthology*
3. Hannah Whitall Smith, *The Christian's Secret to a Happy Life*
4. Andrew Murray, *Abide in Christ*
5. Thomas Merton, *No Man Is an Island*
6. Brother Lawrence, *The Practice of the Presence of God*

7. E. Stanley Jones, *Abundant Living*
8. A. W. Tozer, *The Pursuit of God*
9. Søren Kierkegaard, *Training in Christianity*
10. Julian of Norwich, *Revelations of Divine Love*

Christianity and Business
1. Richard C. Chewning, John W. Eby, and Shirley J. Roels, *Business Through the Eyes of Faith*
2. James R. Hind, *The Heart and Soul of Effective Management: A Christian Approach to Managing and Motivating People*
3. Oliver F. Williams and John W. Houck, *The Judeo-Christian Vision and the Modern Corporation*
4. Oliver F. Williams and John W. Houck, *Full Value: Cases in Christian Business Ethics*
5. Donald Seibert, *The Ethical Executive*
6. Max Depree, *Leadership Is an Art*
7. John H. Redekop, ed., *Labor Problems in Christian Perspective*

Christianity and Creativity
1. Dorothy L. Sayers, *The Mind of the Maker*
2. Elizabeth O'Connor, *Eighth Day of Creation: Gifts and Creativity*
3. D. Bruce Lockerbie, *The Timeless Moment: Creativity and the Christian Faith*

Christianity and Cross-Cultural Communication
1. E. Stanley Jones, *The Christ of the Indian Road*
2. Ralph E. Dodge, *The Revolutionary Bishop Who Saw God at Work in Africa*
3. Elias Chacour with David Hazard, *Blood Brothers*
4. Paul D. Clasper, *Eastern Paths and the Christian Way*
5. Norman B. Rohrer, *Open Arms*

Christianity and the Cults
1. William J. Petersen, *Those Curious New Cults*

Christianity and Culture
1. Malcolm Muggeridge, *Christ and the Media*
2. Ken Myers, *All God's Children and Blue Suede Shoes: Christians and Popular Culture*
3. H. Richard Niebuhr, *Christ and Culture*
4. Francis Schaeffer, *The God Who Is There*
5. Paul Johnson, *Intellectuals*
6. Tony Campolo, *We Have Met the Emeny and They Are Partly Right*
7. Carl F. H. Henry, *Twilight of a Great Civilization*
8. Charles Colson, *Against the Night*
9. Quentin J. Schultze, *American Evangelicals and the Mass Media*
10. Quentin J. Schultze, *Redeeming Television*
11. Lloyd Billingsley, *The Seductive Image: A Christian Critique of the World of Film*
12. Gary Warner, *Out to Win*

Christianity and Drama
1. Nigel Forde, *Theatercraft: Creativity and the Art of Drama*
2. Oliver Hubbard, *"A Critical Analysis of Selected American Dramas (1950–1975) in Light of the Christian View of Man"*
3. Tom Driver, *Romantic Quest and Modern Query*
4. Baker's Plays, *Catalog of Religious Plays*
5. Nelvin Vos, *The Great Pendulum of Becoming*

Christianity and Economics
1. Brian Griffiths, *The Creation of Wealth: A Christian's Case for Capitalism*
2. Bob Goudzwaard, *Idols of Our Time*
3. Jim Halteman, *Market Capitalism and Christianity*
4. Arthur Simon, *Bread for the World*

5. Carl Kreider, *The Rich and the Poor: A Christian Perspective on Global Economics*

Christianity and Education
1. Arthur Holmes, *The Idea of a Christian College*
2. Elton Trueblood, *The Idea of a College*
3. William Ringenberg, *The Christian College: A History of Protestant Higher Education in America*
4. D. Bruce Lockerbie, *Thinking and Acting Like a Christian*
5. Nicholas Wolterstorff, *Educating for Responsible Action*

Christianity and the Environment
1. Herman E. Daly and John B. Cobb, Jr., *For the Common Good*
2. Frances Schaeffer, *Pollution and the Death of Man*
3. Loren Wilkinson, *Earthkeeping in the Nineties*

Christianity and Excellence
1. Edward Dayton and Ted Engstrom, *Strategy for Living: How to Make the Best Use of Your Time and Abilities*

Christianity and the Family
1. Lewis Smedes, *Caring and Commitment: Learning to Live the Love We Promise*
2. Charles P. De Santo and Terri R. Williams, *Putting Love to Work in Marriage*
3. Jay Kesler, *Ten Mistakes Parents Make with Teenagers (And How to Avoid Them)*
4. James Dobson, *Dare to Discipline*
5. James Dobson, *The Strong-Willed Child*
6. H. Wayne House, ed., *Divorce and Remarriage: Four Christian Views*
7. Archibald D. Hart, *Children and Divorce: What to Expect, How to Help*
8. Robert Coles, *The Spiritual Life of Children*

9. Walter Wangerin, *As for Me and My House*
10. Marilee P. Dunker, *Days of Glory, Seasons of Night*

Christianity and the Fine Arts
1. Roger Hazelton, *A Theological Approach to Art*
2. Leland Ryken, ed., *The Christian Imagination: Essays on Literature and the Arts*
3. Calvin Seerveld, *Rainbows for the Fallen World: Aesthetic Life and Artistic Task*
4. Calvin Seerveld, *A Christian Critique of Art*
5. Madeleine L'Engle, *Walking on Water: Reflections on Faith and Art*
6. Don Whittle, *Christianity and the Arts*
7. Nicholas Wolterstorff, *Art in Action*
8. Harold Best, *Music Through the Eyes of Faith*

Christianity and the Future
1. Paul Tournier, *Learn to Grow Old*
2. George Ladd, *The Last Things*
3. Peter Kreeft, *Heaven: The Heart's Deepest Longing*
4. C. S. Lewis, *The Great Divorce*
5. Robert Clouse, ed., *The Meaning of the Millennium: Four Views*
6. Gordon Aeschliman, *Global Trends: Ten Changes Affecting Christians Everywhere*
7. Raymond A. Moody, Jr., *Life after Life*

Christianity and History
1. Herbert Butterfield, *Christianity and History*
2. Ron Wells, *History Through the Eyes of Faith*
3. C. T. McIntire, *God, History, and Historians*
4. George Marsden and Frank Roberts, *A Christian View of History?*
5. Donald Dayton, *Discovering an Evangelical Heritage*

6. Mark Noll, George Marsden, and Nathan Hatch, *The Search for Christian America*
7. Bruce Shelley, *Church History in Plain Language*

Christianity and Humor
1. Elton Trueblood, *The Humor of Christ*
2. Tom Mullen, *Laughing Out Loud and Other Religious Experiences*
3. Conrad Hyers, ed., *Holy Laughter*

Christianity and the Idea of God
1. A. W. Tozer, *The Knowledge of the Holy*
2. J. B. Phillips, *Your God Is Too Small*
3. J. I. Packer, *Knowing God*
4. Hugh Ross, *The Fingerprints of God*

Christianity and International Relations
1. Roland Bainton, *Christian Attitudes Toward War and Peace*

Christianity and Leadership
1. Ted Engstrom, *The Making of a Christian Leader*

Christianity and Learning
1. James Sire, *Discipleship of the Mind*
2. Harry Blamires, *The Christian Mind*
3. John R. Stott, *Your Mind Matters*

Christianity and Lifestyle
1. Vernand Eller, *The Simple Life*
2. Tom Sine, *Why Settle for More and Miss the Best?*

Christianity and Literature
1. Susan V. Gallagher and Roger Lundin, *Literature Through the Eyes of Faith*
2. D. Bruce Lockerbie, *The Liberating Word: Art and the Mystery of the Gospel*

3. Leland Ryken, *Triumphs of the Imagination: Literature in Christian Perspective*
4. Fyodor Dostoyevsky, *Crime and Punishment*
5. Chaim Potok, *The Chosen*
6. Herman Melville, *Moby Dick*
7. Graham Greene, *The End of the Affair*
8. John Updike, *Rabbit Run*
9. Frederick Buechner, *Telling the Truth: The Gospel As Tragedy, Comedy, and Fairy Tale*
10. Merle Meeter, compiler, *The Country of the Risen King: An Anthology of Christian Poetry*
11. Flannery O'Connor, *Mystery and Manners*
12. Stuart Barton Babbage, *The Mark of Cain: Studies in Literature and Theology*
13. *The New Oxford Book of English Verse*
14. Luci Shaw, *A Widening Light: Poems of the Incarnation*
15. G. B. Tennyson and Edward E. Ericson, Jr., eds., *Religion and Modern Literature: Essays in Theory and Criticism*
16. George Herbert, *The Temple*
17. Zola Neale Hurston, *Their Eyes Were Watching God*
18. T. S. Eliot, *Murder in the Cathedral*
19. Walker Percy, *Love in the Ruins*
20. Leo Tolstoy, *Anna Karenina*
21. Leo Tolstoy, *The Death of Ivan Ilych*
22. Sally McFague, *Literature in the Christian Life*
23. Dorothy L. Sayers, *The Man Born to Be King*

Christianity and Meaning

1. David L. Neuhouser, "Open to Reason" (available in the Taylor University library directly or by interlibrary loan)
2. Viktor Frankl, *Man's Search for Meaning*
3. Charles Swindoll, *Living on the Ragged Edge*

Christianity and Mental and Physical Health

1. Lewis Smedes, *Forgive and Forget: Healing the Hurts We Don't Deserve*

2. David Seamands, *Healing for Damaged Emotions*
3. David Augsburger, *Caring Enough to Forgive*
4. Paul Tournier, *The Violence Within*
5. Bernie S. Siegel, *Love, Medicine and Miracles*
6. E. Stanley Jones, *Is the Kingdom of God Realism?*
7. Charles T. Kuntzleman, *The Well Family Book*
8. Ronald M. Enroth, *Churches That Abuse*
9. Archibald D. Hart, *Coping with Depression in the Ministry and Other Helping Professions*
10. Archibald D. Hart, *Depression: Coping and Caring*
11. Matthew Linn, Sheila Fabricant, and Dennis Linn, *Healing the Eight Stages of Life*

Christianity and the Modern Evangelical Faith
1. Richard Quebedeaux, *The Young Evangelicals*

Christianity and the Need to Belong
1. Eric Hoffer, *The True Believer*

Christianity and the Occult
1. Kurt Koch, *Christian Counseling and Occultism*
2. Frank E. Peretti, *This Present Darkness* and *Piercing the Darkness*
3. McCandlish Phillips, *The Spirit World*
4. Timothy Warner, *Spiritual Warfare*

Christianity and the Open Mind
1. Gordon Allport, *The Nature of Prejudice*
2. Arthur Holmes, *All Truth Is God's Truth*
3. Os Guinness, *The Gravedigger File*
4. David Gill, *The Opening of the Christian Mind*

Christianity and Other World Views
1. James Sire, *The Universe Next Door*
2. Martin Buber, *Two Types of Faith*

3. Bertrand Russell, *Why I Am Not a Christian*
4. William Barrett, *Irrational Man: A Study in Existential Philosophy*

Christianity and Personal Confidence
1. Brennan Manning, *Lion and Lamb: The Relentless Tenderness of Jesus*
2. Bill Gillham and Preston H. Gillham, *Lifetime Guarantee*
3. Neil Anderson, *Victory Over the Darkness*

Christianity and Philosophy
1. Arthur F. Holmes, *Ethics: Approaching Moral Decisions*
2. Søren Kierkegaard, *Either-Or*
3. Winfried Courduan, *Mysticism: An Evangelical Option*
4. Nicholas Wolterstorff, *Reason Within the Bounds of Religion*

Christianity and Political Science
1. Robert B. Fowler, *A New Engagement: Evangelical Political Thought, 1966–1976.*
2. Augustus Cerillo, Jr., and Murray W. Dempster, *Salt and Light: Evangelical Political Thought in Modern America*
3. Mark Hatfield, *Between a Rock and a Hard Place*
4. Richard J. Mouw, *Politics and the Biblical Drama*
5. Glenn Tinder, *The Political Meaning of Christianity*
6. Jacques Ellul, *The Politics of God and the Politics of Man*

Christianity and the Problem of Evil
1. C. S. Lewis, *The Problem of Pain*
2. C. S. Lewis, *The Screwtape Letters*
3. Philip Yancey, *Where Is God When It Hurts?*
4. Paul R. House, *The Unity of the Twelve*
5. Annie Dillard, *Holy the Firm*

Christianity and Providence
1. Leslie Weatherhead, *The Will of God*
2. Philip Yancey, *Disappointment with God*

Christianity and Psychology
1. John White, *Putting the Soul Back in Psychology*
2. Karl Menninger, *Whatever Became of Sin?*
3. Paul Vitz, *Psychology As Religion: The Cult of Self-Worship*
4. David G. Myers and Malcolm A. Jeeves, *Psychology Through the Eyes of Faith*
5. Robert Coles, *Harvard Diary: Reflections on the Sacred and the Secular*
6. Stan Jones, ed., *Psychology and the Christian Faith*

Christianity and Science
1. Richard Bube, *The Human Quest*
2. Denis Alexander, *Beyond Science*
3. Mark Cosgrove, *The Amazing Body Human*
4. Richard T. Wright, *Biology Through the Eyes of Faith*
5. Paul Brand and Philip Yancey, *Fearfully and Wonderfully Made*
6. Annie Dillard, *Pilgrim at Tinker Creek*

Christianity and Self-Worth
1. Paul Tournier, *The Strong and the Weak*
2. James Dobson, *Hide or Seek*

Christianity and Sexuality
1. Lewis Smedes, *Sex for Christians*
2. Josh McDowell and Dick Day, *Why Wait?*
3. Letha Scanzoni, *Why Wait: A Christian View of Premarital Sex*

Christianity and Society
1. Alan Paton, *Cry, the Beloved Country*
2. Thomas More, *Utopia*
3. John Perkins, *With Justice Toward All*
4. Harriet Beecher Stowe, *Uncle Tom's Cabin*
5. Nicholas Wolterstorff, *Until Justice and Peace Embrace*
6. Garth Lean, *God's Politician: William Wilberforce's Struggle*

7. Tony Campolo and David Fraser, *Sociology Through the Eyes of Faith*

Christianity and Theological Systems
1. William Hordern, *A Layman's Guide to Protestant Theology*

Christianity and Vocation
1. Arthur F. Miller and Ralph T. Mattson, *The Truth About You: Discover What You Should be Doing With Your Life*
2. Richard B. Bolles, *What Color Is Your Parachute?*
3. Leland Ryken, *Christian Perspectives on Work and Leisure*
4. John Bernbaum and Simon Steer, *Why Work? Careers and Employment in Biblical Perspective*

Christianity and the World
1. Jacques Ellul, *The Presence of the Kingdom*
2. John Bright, *Kingdom of God*

Other Bibliographies of Christian Literature
1. Beatrice Batson, *A Reader's Guide to Religious Literature*
2. Mark L. Branson, ed., *The Reader's Guide to the Best Evangelical Books*
3. Harish D. Merchant, ed., *Encounter with Books: A Guide to Christian Reading*
4. Kenneth W. Hermann, ed., *Every Thought Captive to Christ: A Guide to Resources for Developing a Christian Perspective in the Major Academic Disciplines*
5. Jerry Self, ed., *Integrating Faith and Discipline: A Bibliography*